A GUIDE TO

MARKETING LAW

LAW

WHAT EVERY SELLER
SHOULD KNOW

A GUIDE TO
MARKETING
LAW
WHAT EVERY SELLER
SHOULD KNOW

Richard M. Steuer

Law & Business, Inc.
Harcourt Brace Jovanovich, Inc.
New York   Washington, D.C.

Library of Congress Cataloging-in-Publication Data

Steuer, Richard M.
  A guide to marketing law.

  Includes index.
  1. Marketing—Law and legislation—United States.
2. Retail trade—Law and legislation—United States.
I. Title.
KF2005.S74 1985   343.73'084   85-24065
ISBN 0-15-004404-6   347.30384

to Milton Handler

CONTENTS

Marketing executives consult their lawyers for pieces of advice on many occasions, but they seldom have time to engage in any comprehensive examination of the laws with which they have to contend. This book is designed to provide just that kind of overview. It offers practical suggestions for structuring and implementing marketing decisions in ways that will minimize legal risks. It also waves some red flags, identifying the types of situations in which it is important to consult a lawyer before taking action. Even the executive with no time to attend law courses or seminars can read through this book and become conversant with the basic legal principles in short order.

One of the most satisfying aspects of practicing law on behalf of companies engaged in marketing is strategic counselling, to help find lawful, low-risk avenues for achieving marketing objectives. One of the most frustrating experiences is to be called in too late, when a court battle which could have been avoided has already begun, because someone in the organization did not know the law and failed to recognize a potential problem in time.

My objective in writing this book has been to help prevent such blunders by bridging the gap between marketing and the law. Marketing executives who understand the full spectrum of legal fundamentals will be alert to the need for advice when it is required, and will be better equipped to act on that advice once it is given. If marketing executives and their lawyers can speak each other's language, they will be less likely to talk past one another when a crisis arises. That kind of improvement in communication is what this book is meant to accomplish.

Richard M. Steuer
New York City
July, 1985

ACKNOWLEDGEMENTS

I am grateful for the support and assistance of a number of my colleagues in bringing this project to fulfillment. Joshua Greenberg was kind enough to review the entire manuscript and make a host of insightful suggestions. Chris Brewster and Howard Shire generously shared their special expertise. I am also grateful to all of those clients who, in a very real sense, have continually afforded me the most valuable opportunities to educate myself in the intricacies and the practicalities of marketing law.

Special thanks go to my wife, Audrey, and to the rest of my family for their continuing patience, encouragement and good humor.

INTRODUCTION

Some of the most frequent visitors to the legal departments of America's corporations are marketing executives. From the vice president to the district manager, most marketing leaders are veterans of more than a few legal entanglements.

This book is designed to introduce marketing executives to the law which lurks about them, and to suggest some approaches for reducing exposure to lawsuits and liability. It is no substitute for firsthand advice from a knowledgeable lawyer, but it can explain when to seek such advice, and why. It also can help to prepare for those inevitable encounters when a judgment must be made "on your own," before there is any opportunity to consult an attorney at all.

Obviously, a book of this kind cannot provide an in-depth analysis of every legal issue which marketing presents. This is not a legal encyclopedia. What it can provide is an overview, and in the process it may spark consultations with lawyers concerning subjects which might otherwise be overlooked. Ideally, this can lead to practical solutions which not only resolve thorny problems, but avert needless litigation. In some situations there is no room to maneuver and legal confrontation is inevitable, but in most situations a well-prepared marketing executive can structure decisions in a manner that will avoid litigation without sacrificing the desired goals.

Lawyers can use this book too. For the lawyer who is new

to the field, this book can provide a concise introduction to the basic principles without overwhelming details and citations. For the lawyer who advises in this area regularly, it can be used to open up better lines of communication with clients, affording the client a greater understanding of where the lawyer is "coming from."

The book is divided into eight chapters. The first gives an outline of the most important marketing statutes and other essentials. The second is a "how-to" manual for launching a distribution network and adding new dealers. Chapter Three provides instructions for spelling out the dealers' and suppliers' respective obligations. Chapter Four explains how to end unhappy distribution relationships.

The fifth chapter is a legal survival kit for making pricing decisions and running promotions. The sixth describes the legal "ABC's" of advertising and selling. Chapter Seven outlines the law which applies to new product development, including trademarks and patents. The final chapter covers the laws that protect consumers and govern consumer relations.

Together, these areas constitute the legal environment in which marketing executives must endeavor to compete and succeed. The executive who understands what the law demands and what the law allows will have a head start in this pursuit.

One

THE
GROUND
RULES

If there is purgatory for marketing executives, it probably resembles the reception area of a legal department or law office. There, the executive spends what seems like an eternity mulling over how he is going to explain to the lawyers and his boss why he wrote that memo, terminated that account, or offered those discounts. "If only I knew the rules," he mutters over and over. He should have read this book.

STAYING OUT OF COURT

There is no shortage of painful tales about marketing executives caught in the web of litigation. The process can be costly, even if the lawsuits eventually are won. Long hours of executive time must be devoted to preparation and testifying. Thousands of sensitive documents may need to be turned over. Simply having to publish descriptions of certain lawsuits in annual reports and other disclosure materials can have an adverse effect on a company's reputation. And lawyers' fees, experts' fees and other litigation costs can mount for years.

The solution, of course, is to avoid getting sued, and to make sure that if you are sued, the case will be thrown out in short order. But this requires some notion of what the law permits, what it forbids, and when to seek advice. You cannot always rely on your instincts, because the law is full of surprises. And you have to use common sense.

The alternative is to leap into the abyss, and hope that you don't land in court. Consider, for example, the salesman who received material from one of his company's pharmaceutical dealers, indicating that another dealer was not complying with company policy. The salesman sent the material on to his district manager, and shot off this covering memorandum: "His motivation for leaving this with me? I'm sure he knows I'll send it along and subsequently, another nail in [the other dealer's] box!!" The other dealer was later terminated, and sued the company and the first dealer for conspiring to cut him off. The memo became the principal piece of evidence, and a jury awarded damages. An appeals court ultimately reversed, holding that the memo did not prove that there had been any conspiracy, but not before more than five years of litigation had gone by.

Also consider the furniture executive who was faced with a complaint from his largest customer, a department store chain. The chain was upset with a dealer in Denver who was advertising cut-rate prices, and comparing them with the chain's prices. The executive telephoned the dealer and said, "I'd like to know what needs to be done, Tom, to stop a price war—what you want from us or what you expect from us." He added that he already had "extracted a promise" from a third outlet in Denver "that he'd get his prices up and keep them up, which is illegal to even talk about." What the executive didn't know was that the dealer on the other end was recording their conversation. In a flash, the tape became the first exhibit presented to the jury in the dealer's lawsuit.

You needn't be an "unguided missile" to wind up in court. Consider the executives who reasoned that they could sell their prefabricated homes to a customer by offering favorable credit terms. The customer later sued, charging that he had been compelled to buy from this seller because no one else offered such attractive rates. The executives' company spent fifteen years in litigation, with two trips to the United States Supreme Court, before being vindicated.

And executives are not the only ones who find themselves in litigation. Don't overlook the astronaut who endorsed an automotive product that was supposed to provide better mileage. He was sued by the Federal Trade Commission, which claimed that the product didn't work.

The consequences of losing a litigation can be bitter, and are not limited to cash outlays, although these can reach millions of dollars. Consider the owners of the one-time trademarks for "escalator" and "thermos," who lost the exclusive rights to these names forever because they were unable to prevent them from becoming generic.

And don't forget the executives who went to jail for agreeing on prices in the electrical equipment industry. The judge refused to limit their punishment to a fine, later remarking, "I don't think money represented anything to them."

From these illustrations, two ground rules should already be clear: don't be sloppy in writing or conversation; and when in doubt, seek out the advice of a knowledgeable lawyer. Beyond that, it is important to have some basic understanding of the laws which apply to marketing, and how they have been interpreted by the courts.

THE MAJOR STATUTES

This book will not dwell on legalisms or specific pieces of legislation, but a quick summary of the most significant laws pertaining to marketing is necessary in order to put what comes later into some perspective. There is no denying that nothing makes drier reading than statutes. But it's no fun to watch the game if you don't know any of the rules. Hang in there for a few pages of edicts, ordinances and provisos, and the rest of this book will seem like child's play.

The Federal Antitrust Laws.

The most important laws concerning distribution are the federal antitrust laws. Chief among them is the Sherman Act, passed by Congress in 1890. It is a remarkably simple piece of legislation, prohibiting contracts, combinations and conspiracies in restraint of interstate or foreign trade. This means that, for openers, there must be more than one company or individual involved for the Act to apply, and they must have reached some kind of agreement on a common plan.

Shortly after the Sherman Act was adopted, courts began interpreting it to prohibit only "unreasonable" restraints of trade, since a literal application of its language would have outlawed virtually every contract ever written. This standard was dubbed the "rule of reason." Unfortunately, the line which the courts have drawn to divide what is "reasonable" from what is not has shifted considerably over time. It has become something of a running consensus through the years, and this has created no small degree of uncertainty for the business community.

The Sherman Act also prohibits monopolization, attempted monopolization, and conspiracies to monopolize. These prohibitions sometimes limit the marketing activities of firms possessing substantial market power, particularly when it turns out that the firms are bent on destroying would-be competitors. Monopolization and attempted monopolization are the only Sherman Act offenses that can be committed by a single firm, acting alone.

Another important antitrust statute is the Clayton Act, adopted in 1914. This is a more narrowly drawn piece of legislation, which prohibits a number of specific sales practices. It was meant to fill in some of the gaps which Congress thought were left in the Sherman Act. Also of importance is the Robinson-Patman Act, passed in 1936, which prohibits certain price discrimination and discriminatory allowances.

HIGHLIGHTS OF THE ANTITRUST LAWS

Sherman Act (1890)

Section 1: Prohibits contracts, combinations and conspiracies which unreasonably restrain interstate or foreign trade.

Section 2: Prohibits monopolization, attempted monopolization and conspiracies to monopolize.

Clayton Act (1914)

Section 3: Prohibits conditioning the sale or lease of one product on a promise not to purchase competing products (this includes "tying" and "exclusive dealing"), where the effect may be substantially to lessen competition or tend to create a monopoly.

Section 4: Provides for private treble damage actions for violations of the antitrust laws.

Section 7: Prohibits mergers and acquisitions which may substantially lessen competition or tend to create a monopoly.

Section 16: Provides for private suits for injunctive relief under the antitrust laws.

Robinson-Patman Act (1936) (amending the Clayton Act)

Section 2(a): Prohibits price discrimination in specified circumstances.

Section 2(c): Prohibits payment of brokerage, commission or other compensation in connection with a sale except for services rendered.

Section 2(d): Prohibits discrimination in allowances for services or facilities furnished by a customer.

Section 2(e): Prohibits discrimination in furnishing services or facilities to a customer.

Section 2(f): Prohibits inducement or receipt by a buyer of an unlawfully discriminatory price.

Federal Trade Commission Act (1914)
    Section 5:   Prohibits unfair methods of competition
                  and unfair or deceptive acts or practices in
                  or affecting interstate commerce.

Enforcement.

The Justice Department is charged with enforcing the federal antitrust laws, a task assigned to the Department's Antitrust Division. The Division can bring either civil or criminal
cases. Sherman Act violations may be prosecuted as felonies,
punishable by up to three years in prison and a fine of up to
$100,000 for individuals, or by a fine of up to $1 million in the
case of a corporation. In practice, criminal charges normally are
levelled only against the most egregious conduct, principally
price fixing agreements among competitors. Civil cases can also
have profound effects, however, since the courts are empowered to issue injunctions, and these can dramatically limit the
methods by which companies are permitted to market their
products.

Private parties are entitled to sue under the antitrust laws,
and recover three times their actual damages plus attorneys'
fees. This treble damage provision was designed both to encourage private enforcement and to discourage lawbreaking.
Private parties also may obtain injunctive relief.

Federal Trade Commission.

The Federal Trade Commission is responsible for enforcing
the Federal Trade Commission Act, a separate statute passed at
the same time as the Clayton Act, which prohibits "unfair methods of competition" and "unfair or deceptive acts or practices."
The Commission may issue "cease and desist" orders prohibiting particular conduct, and is also authorized to issue blanket
"trade regulation rules" which cover categories of conduct and
are applicable to entire industries. There is no private right to
sue for either damages or injunctions under the FTC Act.

Other Statutes.

Numerous states have enacted their own antitrust laws and "Little FTC Acts," containing a variety of provisions and remedies. There also exists an entirely separate body of law concerning relationships between franchisors and franchisees. This includes federal legislation applicable to service stations and automobile dealers, as well as a broad and not very uniform galaxy of state laws addressing a wider variety of industries.

A few other specific statutes will be described in subsequent chapters as they become relevant, but this outline should be sufficient to provide some basic familiarity with the laws which apply to distribution. Just how these laws affect the decision-making process—and intrude upon the lives of marketing executives—is the subject of the remainder of this book. Sometimes the intrusion of the law is minimal, but sometimes it can be pervasive, as is often the case with relations between suppliers and their dealers. Since the law usually plays so large a role in these relations, it is here that we begin.

Two

ENLISTING DEALERS

Suppliers and their dealers sue one another with alarming frequency. In fact, most of the lawsuits in which marketing executives find themselves on the witness stand these days arise from conflicts between suppliers and dealers.

This should come as no surprise. Tensions within marketing channels are inevitable, since there is a fundamental friction at work between suppliers and dealers over how to divide the profits. The eventual result, all too often, is irritation, resentment, or even outright contempt. How common it is to hear the marketing directors of suppliers refer to certain of their dealers as "mavericks," "bad apples" and "bootleggers," while dealers just as commonly term their suppliers "extortionists," "rapists" and more. The function of the law in these situations is to establish some ground rules to govern distribution channels and to resolve disputes which cannot be disposed of by less formal means.

In this and the following two chapters we will address those unique and stormy romances, marriages, quarrels and divorces which typify relationships between suppliers and their dealers, and try to analyze them in the context of the American legal system.

THE SELECTION PROCESS

Product distribution channels typically include a combination of suppliers, wholesalers and retailers, with these functions sometimes being combined. Often, distribution channels exhibit a life-cycle of sorts. They are created. They evolve. Eventually, they may dissolve. At each step along the way the law can intrude to nullify or modify a company's decisions, and it is important to know the rules.

Creation of a distribution channel by a manufacturer, importer, or other supplier naturally requires the initial selection of dealers, including both wholesalers and retailers. Ordinarily, this does not present any legal dilemmas. This is one instance in which the law allows the supplier to exercise considerable discretion.

Suppliers apply a wide array of criteria in choosing their dealers, of course, depending upon the type of product involved and the economic strength of the supplier himself. Some products, such as toothpaste, require widespread distribution with virtually no consumer services (such as demonstrations or repairs) and relatively little attention to the retailer's image. Other products, such as stereo equipment, call for more limited distribution, with heavy reliance on the dealers for salesmanship and service, and with more emphasis on the retailer's image. These criteria dictate the number and types of dealers the supplier will endeavor to recruit.

The supplier's success in persuading dealers to sign on will be determined largely by the magnitude of the investment each dealer is required to make (in inventory, facilities, personnel and promotional effort), the degree of economic muscle the supplier wields in the market (is he a struggling newcomer or an established powerhouse, for example), and, of course, the inherent appeal of the product itself (although this may be the most difficult factor for a potential dealer to judge, at least at the time a new product is being introduced).

Under the law, the supplier is afforded broad latitude in selecting those dealers whom he expects to do the best job of selling his product. The supplier may, for instance, choose dealers who he anticipates will display and demonstrate his products, vigorously advertise and promote them, adequately service them, and convey the appropriate image. Other common criteria include the dealer's creditworthiness, reputation for honesty, and compatibility with the supplier's own personnel. Naturally, the relative importance of each of these criteria will vary sharply, depending upon what type of product is involved, whether the particular dealer is a wholesaler or a retailer, and the supplier's overall marketing strategy.

Whatever their relative importance, however, these are all legitimate considerations under the law, and each supplier may apply them as he sees fit in selecting his dealers. These are the relatively easy decisions for the supplier to make, at least from a legal perspective.

DISCOUNTERS

The harder question in selecting dealers is how to handle so-called "discounters"—those dealers who regularly sell at less than the resale prices which suppliers suggest or which other dealers customarily charge. Even suppliers who have never dreamt of selling through discounters commonly will be approached by discounters from time to time seeking to establish a relationship. Such suppliers also may find that some of their old, established dealers, who may never have engaged in discounting before, will begin to discount one day, either to meet new competition, to combat falling sales or for other reasons.

Since the early part of this century, the courts have prohibited suppliers from requiring their dealers to charge a fixed resale price. Underlying this rule is the theory that discounting stirs up competition and affords consumers lower prices. Fixing resale prices (sometimes termed "resale price maintenance") is flat out against the law.

The only question today is whether the law should be changed. The so-called "Chicago School" economic theories,

which are being increasingly cited by the courts, point out that
the presence of discounters in a distribution network can make
it difficult to attract and retain other dealers who provide more
extensive customer services but must charge higher prices in order to cover their higher overhead. There are strongly held
views on both sides of this issue, and the philosophical debate
is ongoing. Some observers believe that eventually the law will
come around to the "Chicago" view, and that fixing retail prices
will not necessarily be illegal, but it would be premature to rely
on such predictions today.

Congress itself has shifted ground on the subject of discounting over the years, as has the Justice Department. In 1937
Congress authorized the states to permit suppliers to prohibit
discounting by enacting "Fair Trade Laws." Congress repealed
this legislation in 1975, however, and the Fair Trade Laws,
which had been adopted at one time or another in forty-six
states, disappeared. The Justice Department, taking an almost
countercyclical approach, historically sought to protect discounters, but more recently has embraced the position that manufacturers may well have a legitimate right to discourage
discounting.

What, you may ask, does all of this history have to do with
the price of eggs? In fact, it has everything to do with it, and
with all retail prices. Discounting has been as much a political
football as a legal or economic issue. Lobbying has been intense
both for and against discounters, and the conflict is not likely to
go away for good regardless of how it is resolved at any point
in time.

Through all of this vacillation and conflict, however, one
thing has always remained clear: the supplier has the right to
refuse to *begin* dealing with known discounters, either at the
time of forming a new distribution network or later on. A supplier is not obligated to provide an open door for discounters
when he sets up or adds to his system of distribution, and those
are the best times for the supplier to decide whether he wants
to sell through discounters or not.

Once a dealer has been welcomed into a distribution network, the picture changes dramatically. Forcing existing dealers

to *agree* not to engage in any discounting in the future is illegal—despite the fact that it is not illegal to refuse to begin dealing with known discounters in the first place.

The logical inconsistency here has not escaped notice, but this is where the courts have chosen to draw the line. This line permits a supplier to choose his own dealers without the courts second-guessing his motives for refusing to select particular candidates. At the same time, it forbids suppliers from forcing their dealers to promise not to cut prices after the dealers have begun carrying their products. This does not mean, however (and this is a big "however"), that dealers may begin discounting at the cost of sacrificing marketing services which the supplier reasonably requires them to provide.

The Colgate Case.

The derivation of this approach is the 1919 decision of the United States Supreme Court in the case of *United States* v. *Colgate & Co.** This is one of very few cases which will be mentioned by name in this book, but it is a watershed for marketing law and worth remembering. The Court held that a supplier is permitted to announce in advance that he will not deal with discounters. Subsequent cases make clear, however, that the supplier is not permitted to pressure dealers into agreeing to adhere to specified resale prices by employing other tactics such as threats of termination, or termination followed by reinstatement on the condition that the dealer reform.

For years there had been disagreement whether, under the *Colgate* doctrine, it would be permissible for a supplier simply to terminate an existing dealer who begins discounting, without entering into any agreement with the dealer to refrain from discounting. It is now clear that suppliers not only may refuse to deal with known discounters initially, but may also terminate their sales to dealers who become discounters later on, *provided*

---

*Citations to the cases referred to throughout the text appear in the Table of Authorities at the back of this volume.

(and this is critical) that the supplier does not engage in any other conduct actually forcing any of his dealers to *agree* to adhere to the desired pricing structure.

In other words, a new supplier rolling out a line of electronic gizmos may announce that he will have nothing to do with discounters, and proceed to limit his sales to dealers with reputations for selling at list price. If some of these dealers unexpectedly begin discounting, the supplier may stop doing business with them outright, so long as there are no special state or federal franchising laws which apply to limit such actions, or other contractual rights which would be violated. The supplier should not, however, first try to pressure his dealers to agree to stop discounting and then terminate those who refuse, or relent later and agree to reinstate them if they promise to conform. Either of these situations can be considered price-fixing conspiracies, and be held unlawful. And the supplier should not seek agreements from his other dealers to keep prices up, because this is illegal too.

The narrowly limited scenario which is permitted under this standard may seem unrealistic to the point of being downright useless. In the real world (which many marketing executives believe has never been visited by travellers from the legal profession), few, if any, suppliers are willing or able to limit themselves to announcing a pricing policy in advance and then cleanly terminating those dealers who begin discounting, without an opportunity for conciliation and without any room for reconsideration. Because of this, the utility of the *Colgate* doctrine is limited when it comes to terminations. Nevertheless, the doctrine unquestionably has the practical value of allowing suppliers to refuse to *begin* dealing with discounters before any relationship is established at all.

TURNING DOWN A DISCOUNTER

What happens, then, when "Dick's Discount Paradise" calls a supplier who has a policy of not dealing with discounters, and asks to be taken on as a dealer? The supplier, after checking with his lawyer, may choose to put his response in writing. This will provide hard evidence of what actually transpired should there be litigation later on. The message should be clear and to the point, as illustrated by **Form 1,** which is an example of the type of letter which can be sent. A copy of any such letter should be retained in case "Dick's" sues.

Of course, many suppliers affirmatively desire to do business with discounters, and make discounters an integral part of their marketing strategy. Economists have pointed out that most suppliers rationally should want their products retailed at

FORM 1
REJECTION LETTER TO WOULD-BE DEALER

```
CERTIFIED MAIL
RETURN RECEIPT REQUESTED

Dick's Discount Paradise
100 Main Street
Anywhere, U.S.A. 12345

Dear Dick:

     Please be advised that we have decided not
to sell our products to you at this time. You
should understand that we, like any other com-
pany, have the right to select our customers, and
the right not to sell to everyone who requests
our merchandise.

                    Very truly yours,


                    _____
```

the lowest possible price in order to generate the greatest consumer demand. Courts generally have understood this to be
true, but at the same time have recognized that discounting may
result in some other dealers withdrawing their promotional or
servicing support, or abandoning the brand altogether. Discounting is not desirable to the supplier in these situations, and
many suppliers prefer to avoid discounters for this reason to the
extent they lawfully can.

MONOPOLISTS

There has been some debate whether a monopolist should
be under a special obligation to sell to all comers, much like a
public utility, despite the general rule that a supplier can sell to
whomever he chooses. The term "monopolist" in this context
is not limited to companies which control 100 percent of a market, like a water company. Instead, the courts have defined a
monopolist as a company with such a high share of the market
(usually over 70 percent) that it can virtually disregard other
sellers in setting its prices, or can drive competitors from the
market if it so chooses.

The "public utility" approach has not been widely accepted, but some cases have suggested that monopolists or
near-monopolists are under a higher duty than others to supply
all dealers who wish to carry their products. Suppliers who are
dominant enough to fall within this charmed circle must take
care that when they refuse to begin dealing with a would-be
dealer, they are not taking this action with the purpose of creating or cementing monopoly power. This is a very vague concept, to be sure, but courts try to apply it. At the same time, it
is also clear that simply because a supplier is in the position of
being a "monopolist," he is not disqualified from exercising his
reasonable business judgment in selecting his dealers. A monopolist may refuse to supply prospective dealers for the same
types of legitimate reasons as any other supplier.

COLLECTIVE REFUSALS TO DEAL

One final caution on selecting distributors: the supplier's decision should be made unilaterally. It is common for suppliers to receive unsolicited advice from existing dealers on the advisability of bringing additional dealers on board. This advice is almost invariably negative, unless the proposed new dealers are slated to be owned by some of the old dealers. Dealers may say things like: "There are enough dealers already. I deserve some protection. This new fellow runs a shabby operation. He slashes prices. If you make him a dealer I'm going to look for another brand." When this type of advice is received by a supplier, an immediate trip to the legal department is in order. The experience of Yamaha a few years ago illustrates the problem.

CASE HISTORY: Listening to Stereo Dealers.

Yamaha introduced a line of stereo equipment in the United States which enjoyed dramatic sales increases during the mid-1970's. It sold these products through franchised dealers, each of whom entered into a written agreement promising to promote Yamaha products at least as much as any competing line, and promising to employ qualified sales personnel. Each dealer also agreed to provide adequate display and demonstration facilities, including at least one separate "sound room" devoted entirely to Yamaha merchandise.

Yamaha selected only a limited number of dealers to serve each area of the country. In Manhattan, it had just two dealers, but as the line caught on, interest in carrying it began to grow.

Borger's was a Manhattan discount hardware and appliance store which was run by two brothers. In 1972, one of their sons, who apparently was something of an audiophile, joined the business and convinced the others to move heavily into sales of stereo equipment. At first, Borger's offered substantial discounts on these products, and advertised heavily that it was slashing manufacturers' suggested retail prices. The lines it was carrying at that time were available everywhere, however, often at low prices, and therefore provided opportunities only for relatively low profit margins.

Borger's became unhappy about its low profits, and decided to search out brands which believed in more limited distribution, making for less competition among their own dealers, and permitting each dealer to realize higher profit margins. In order to attract these brands, Borger's opened an entirely new store in 1976 on the other side of town, staffed by experienced sales personnel and featuring first class display areas, sound rooms and service facilities. It also discontinued advertising large discounts.

At the same time, Borger's approached a number of suppliers engaged in limited distribution, including Yamaha. Several of these suppliers, such as Advent and Mitsubishi, began doing business with Borger's. Yamaha's national sales manager and its Eastern regional manager met with Borger's at the 1976 Consumer Electronics Show in Chicago, and a Yamaha representative subsequently inspected Borger's new facility in Manhattan. This was followed by a personal visit from Yamaha's new regional manager, who toured the premises and then ran through the requirements of a Yamaha franchise agreement.

Soon after this tour, the regional manager telephoned each of the two Yamaha dealers who were already doing business in Manhattan to discuss the possible addition of Borger's as an authorized outlet. Yamaha called this procedure a "dealer canvass," and a canvass of this kind was routinely conducted by telephoning the dealers involved or by actually visiting them. Not surprisingly, neither of the Manhattan dealers was particularly enthusiastic over the prospect of adding a third competitor. Borger's was later informed that because of the negative reaction encountered from the two existing dealers, Borger's would not be approved as a Yamaha franchisee.

Borger's sued, and the controversy raised some interesting issues:

1. Was Yamaha within its rights to have consulted in advance with its two existing dealers? What if it had consulted with the two of them together, in a joint meeting or conference call?

2. Was Yamaha just knuckling under to its other dealers' reluctance to have more competition in Manhattan? Was Yamaha

exercising its own business judgment or was it really conspiring with its other dealers? Was Borger's past history of discounting a factor in Yamaha's decision?

These are tough questions. Yet nothing in these facts constitutes proof that Yamaha was doing anything more than exercising its own judgment, after taking soundings from two of its dealers. Yamaha won this case, because Borger's was unable to prove its allegation that there had been a conspiracy among Yamaha and its existing dealers to exclude discounters and maintain high prices.

HANDLING ALLEGATIONS OF CONSPIRACY

Yamaha's story dramatizes the kind of situation in which allegations of conspiracy are likely to arise. Every time an incident such as this results in a lawsuit, the outcome will depend largely on evidence of the supplier's intent, including letters, internal memoranda and testimony describing conversations among the parties. The danger in a case like this is that the very communication between the supplier and the existing dealers may be viewed as circumstantial evidence of an anticompetitive conspiracy. The Supreme Court recently made it clear in the case of *Monsanto* v. *Spray Rite* that this kind of evidence alone is *not* sufficient to support an inference of conspiracy, but together with other evidence, it still may spell trouble. If a supplier refuses to add a prospective dealer after an existing dealer has advised him not to, a jury months or years later may look at this fact in connection with other evidence and conclude that this refusal was the result of an illegal conspiracy to protect the existing dealer from competition—even if the supplier never really had any intention of adding that new dealer in the first place. It is an ironic dilemma that in some instances a supplier who genuinely does not want to add a would-be dealer may become hesitant to reject him for no other reason than that an existing dealer has been in contact to urge that very course of action.

An easier situation exists in the case of "exclusive distributorships," where the supplier guarantees a single dealer that
no other dealers will be appointed for the same territory. If a
valid exclusive distributorship has been granted to a dealer, that
dealer is entitled to assert his right of exclusivity against any attempt by the supplier to appoint an additional dealer in the
same territory.

RESPONDING TO COMPLAINTS

What is the supplier to do if a dealer who has no exclusive
distributorship contacts the supplier to complain about the
prospect of adding another dealer? The supplier can still write
to the prospective dealer, along the lines indicated in **Form 1,**
turning down the request, but first he should contact the complaining dealer, making it clear that this decision is being made
solely by the supplier himself. An example of such a letter is illustrated by **Form 2.** These letters should be short and sweet,
and not designed to prompt a dialogue.

If more than one of the supplier's existing dealers join together in a concerted effort to block the addition of new dealers,
this in itself may constitute an unlawful conspiracy. ("All of the
dealers talked about it, and we agree that you shouldn't sell to
Dick's.") The supplier must avoid being drawn into this kind of
conspiracy, and if he makes his decision unilaterally, he need
not be.

For practical purposes, a supplier must expect to receive
comments and advice from his existing dealers with some frequency, and the mere receipt of information from dealers is not
illegal. But the supplier must take pains to insure that in actually
selecting new dealers he can separate his own business judgment from the collective or individual advice of his existing dealers. The supplier may establish a special selection committee,
for example, composed of members of the supplier's management. Such a committee can be charged with selecting new dealers under a formal policy, insulated from direct pressure from

FORM 2
RESPONSE TO COMPLAINING DEALER

```
CERTIFIED MAIL
RETURN RECEIPT REQUESTED

Existing Dealer
101 Main Street
Anywhere, U.S.A. 12345

Dear Dealer:

     I am in receipt of your recommendation that
we should deny the request of Dick's Discount
Paradise to become one of our dealers. As you
know, our selection of dealers has always been
our choice alone. While you have expressed your
concern, we will be making our decision in the
exercise of our own business judgment. Whether
we choose to sell to Dick's or not, this decision
will be made unilaterally.

                         Very truly yours,


                         _____
```

---

the existing dealers. Whatever the mechanism, each supplier must establish his own safeguards and controls, and ensure that they are followed in practice as well as in the policy manual.

The upshot of all this is that when the supplier legitimately exercises his own judgment, the law permits substantial leeway in making the initial selection of dealers. If conspiracies with existing dealers can be avoided, and if no monopoly is being created or strengthened in the process, the supplier may exercise considerable discretion at the selection stage. Once the selections are made, however, a new chapter in the supplier-dealer relationship begins.

Three

STRUCTURING DISTRIBUTION ARRANGEMENTS

Dealer selection, of course, is only the first legal headache involving the relationship between supplier and dealer. Sometimes the most troublesome challenge comes with actually shaping the structure of the channel of distribution, particularly where the supplier desires to exert some degree of control over the manner in which the dealers sell his products. While the initial selection of a cadre of dealers provides the supplier some assurance of where and how the product will be sold, this arrangement is subject to change over time as the dealers themselves evolve. A more lasting option for the supplier is the imposition of contractual restrictions on the dealers' methods of doing business, including both their selling practices and their purchasing practices. You may never draft a distribution agreement yourself, but you ought to know what you can and cannot include in these contracts, to make sure that whoever does prepare them provides you with every advantage.

RESTRICTING DEALERS' SALES

There are a variety of sales restraints which are imposed "vertically" (i.e., by the supplier on sales by wholesale and retail dealers), including restraints on where, to whom, at what

23

price and in what manner the dealers may sell. These sales restraints, with the exception of resale price maintenance, are all
governed by the so-called "rule of reason." This means that
they will be upheld if, on balance, they promote "interbrand
competition" (i.e., competition among different brands) at least
as much as they restrain it (either by limiting "intrabrand competition" among dealers of the same brand, or by fostering collusion among competitors).

"Non-price" vertical sales restraints include what have become known as territorial restraints, customer restraints, location clauses, areas of primary responsibility, profit pass-overs
and sales quotas. Each of these will be described briefly in the
pages which follow, together with examples of the kind of language which lawyers use to impose each type of restraint.

It first should be pointed out that each of these restraints
may operate either as a matter of the supplier's own policy, or
as part of a two-sided contract. Relationships between suppliers
and dealers exist with various degrees of legal formality. Some
suppliers merely sell on invoice, having no formal, extended
agreements with their dealers at all. Dealers who carry their
product simply order them. Other suppliers choose to enter into
written distribution contracts with their dealers, reciting in
some detail the rights and obligations of both sides. This permits the supplier to impose certain requirements and limitations
on the dealers in writing, and to provide the dealers with written assurances. Where an agreement of this kind governs the
dealer's fundamental methods of doing business, including,
usually, the name under which his business is conducted, this
may be considered a "franchise" in some states, triggering special franchise protection laws.

If a supplier does not require any promises on the part of
his dealers, he may consider dispensing with formal distribution agreements and instead issuing a unilateral policy statement, setting forth the terms on which he will begin and
continue doing business with dealers. Such a statement may include many of the same requirements as a typical distribution
agreement, but the dealer is not called upon to sign anything.

In these situations courts still may find that an agreement exists if the dealer communicates his intention to comply, so any restrictions that may raise legal problems should only be included after consultation with a lawyer.

Why Restrict Sales?

Some suppliers place no restrictions at all on the manner in which dealers may sell their products, leaving this entirely to the discretion of each dealer. This often is the case with suppliers located abroad and with small suppliers having little or no market power. It also is the case with many inexpensive products sold on meager margins, regardless of the strength of the supplier.

In other instances, suppliers prefer to place restrictions on where dealers may sell, the kinds of customers to whom they may sell, and the methods by which they may sell. All of these restrictions limit the dealers' discretion in deciding how best to compete with one another, and force the dealers to adhere with some uniformity to the marketing strategy mapped out by the supplier.

At first blush, it may appear counterproductive for a supplier to bar his dealers from pursuing what each one considers his own best marketing tactics. After all, individual initiative and involvement often can generate the greatest commitment and the highest sales. On the other hand, the result of dealer free will can be chaos. Dealers may expend most of their efforts fighting off competition from other dealers of the same brand, rather than focusing their efforts on pitting their supplier's products against those of other brands.

This is particularly true in the case of products which require significant dealer effort. Such effort commonly includes knowledgeable and aggressive salesmanship, costly and carefully targeted promotions, prominent and sizeable displays, or fully equipped and stocked repair facilities. Some products, often those which are new or complicated, or have narrow appeal, require an especially high level of dealer services in order to generate consumer demand. Computer equipment, medical diagnostic equipment, video recorders, exercise machines and hot tubs are all good examples. Buyers will be attracted to the product precisely because they see it displayed and promoted, watch it being demonstrated, and know that they can have it repaired conveniently.

But some dealers may chisel on these efforts and pass along all or part of the money they save in the form of lower prices. This price-cutting can attract business away from those dealers who continue to provide the services and must charge higher prices in order to cover their higher costs. The latter dealers pay to generate the demand while the former dealers take a "free ride" on their efforts. In fact, this phenomenon has been labeled "free riding" by economists, and reliance on the free rider theory has become a prominent feature of contemporary legal analysis in this area.

At first glance it may appear that free riding will stimulate competition by encouraging price wars among dealers of the same brand. This is certainly an attractive prospect for bargain-hunting consumers, at least in the short run. Over time, however, free riding can pose a real threat to competition among different brands. The high-overhead, high-priced dealers are likely to become discouraged and cut back their services or switch their allegiance to other brands. In time, the entire brand, accompanied by fewer services, will become less attractive to consumers and less competitive with other brands in the market.

Free riding can arise in a number of ways. For example, a supplier of personal computers, tennis rackets, stereo components or other products may do business with one dealer in each separately identifiable market in the country, with each dealer maintaining showroom and repair facilities, employing sales representatives and repair personnel, and providing local advertising and other promotion. After a while, one of the dealers may begin soliciting sales in other marketing areas by dispatching his sales representatives there, by direct mail solicitation of customers in those other areas, or by regional or national advertising. This often includes "back of the book" classified advertising in specialty or "enthusiast" type magazines aimed at savvy readers. Interested customers may never have to visit the free-riding dealer at all, since orders often can be taken by mail or telephone, and charged to a credit card. The goods can then be shipped to the customer direct, either by mail or freight.

The "invading" dealer in these situations typically induces customers to buy from him instead of from the local dealer by offering lower prices. He is able to do this because the other dealer already has generated demand for the product through that dealer's own promotional efforts. Customers may have examined the product in the other dealer's showroom and have had their questions answered there. They may have selected the model they needed, or the size, color, or accessories, depending on the type of product. The customers also may have been encouraged to buy the product because they knew that the other, full-service dealer in their area maintained repair facilities where warranty work and other servicing could be performed.

The "invading" dealer takes a free ride on these promotional efforts and these investments in showrooms, repair facilities and personnel by providing none of these efforts, yet making the sales these efforts have generated. He is able to offer the low price largely because he does not have to pay for these services outside his home territory. At the same time, the "invaded" dealers often are obligated by contract to provide these services in order to maintain their relationship with the supplier. To make the situation worse, the invading dealer often targets only those customers who are the most profitable to serve, thereby "skimming the cream" of potential business and cutting into the profits of the "invaded" dealer with particular vengeance.

The problem with free riding then, in terms of competition, is that it discourages the "invaded" dealers from continuing to commit their efforts and resources to competing against other brands and, over time, can result in a diminished level of competition among different brands. Why should any dealer spend his money on promotion when another dealer is likely to ride into town and skim off his best customers? Because of this problem, courts typically have been willing to permit reduction or elimination of competition among dealers of the same brand in order to encourage maximum effort on the part of all the dealers in competing against other brands.

Sales restraints all prevent or inhibit free riding to some degree. Certain of these restrictions forbid dealers from invading the territories or soliciting the customers of neighboring dealers of the same brand, forcing each dealer to focus his efforts on competing against other brands. Certain other restrictions, such as location limitations and assigned areas of "primary responsibility," do not foreclose the possibility of internecine rivalry entirely, but still require each dealer to make the full investment expected of him in his own territory before finding other worlds to conquer. If these restrictions increase competition at least as much as they restrain it, they generally will be found reasonable and lawful. Hewlett-Packard resolved a free rider situation not long ago, and its story illustrates some typical problems and at least one solution.

CASE HISTORY: Wrapping Up a Mail-Order Dealer.

In the rough and tumble personal computer business, some enterprising retailers recognized years ago that they could develop profitable, high-volume mail order businesses on limited investments by selling computer equipment at a discount. Of course, customers had to know exactly what they wanted to order, and returns and service could present difficulties, but many customers found the savings on these high-ticket items sufficiently attractive, on balance, to take the plunge and order by mail or phone.

Among this breed of retailers was Computer Place, which ran a retail store on the California coast, but also built up a discount mail order operation which became an important part of its business. Sales began to sour, however, when a number of computer manufacturers, including Apple, Osborne and Hewlett-Packard, took steps to curtail mail order sales nationwide. Hewlett-Packard, for one, had been receiving complaints from several other dealers, including the large Computerland chain, claiming that the mail order houses were unfairly robbing them of customers they had originally attracted and "pre-sold" on the product through demonstrations, explanations, and persuasion.

In 1982, Hewlett-Packard executives met with representatives of Computerland to address a variety of matters, and in the course of that meeting the mail order situation was discussed. A few months later, Hewlett-Packard introduced a new marketing program. This included an announcement that it had developed a number of new models which would only be distributed through dealers who did not engage in mail order sales.

Computer Place was upset, and thought that it smelled a fix on the part of Computerland. It instituted a lawsuit, raising some difficult questions:

1. Was Hewlett-Packard within its rights to announce that it would not sell its new models to mail order dealers? Could Hewlett-Packard have required its dealers to sign written agreements promising not to sell through the mail? Would such an agreement have amounted to an unreasonable restraint of trade?

2. What if instead, the dealers had agreed only to sell face-to-face to customers who actually visited their stores? Or what if the dealers simply had promised not to sell at a discount from list price?

3. Did the fact that Computer Place was selling at discount prices mean that Hewlett-Packard's actions really amounted to an effort to fix retail prices?

4. Since Hewlett-Packard adopted its new policy after speaking to Computerland, can it be inferred that there was a conspiracy between the two?

Mail order bans are usually lawful if they serve a procompetitive purpose such as elimination of a free rider problem. This is particularly true where the brand has a relatively low market share. The fact that discounting may be discouraged by such a restraint does not, in itself, render the restraint unlawful. As for a supplier consulting its dealers with regard to sales restraints, we have seen that the exchange of information is normally permissible so long as the supplier ultimately makes its own decisions. Hewlett-Packard won this case, having acted decisively to resolve a genuine marketing problem.

When Are Sales Restraints Illegal?

Are sales restraints ever unreasonable? Yes, although the law is becoming increasingly permissive, and it is becoming harder to prove illegality. Today, there remain three principal areas of risk: First, sales restraints still may be held unlawful if they amount to resale price maintenance, or if they at least are bound up with resale price maintenance. Second, they also may be held unlawful if they are purely the brainchild of the dealers, devised to protect the dealers from competition by their confreres, and foisted upon a reluctant supplier. Third, they also may be held unlawful if, on balance, they really don't increase competition as much as they diminish competition, particularly where the dealers do not provide many services to begin with, or the supplier commands a high share of the market.

Resale Price Maintenance.

Taking these hazards in order, resale price maintenance remains *per se* illegal, despite recent criticisms of this rule from several economists and from the Department of Justice itself. If a sales restraint actually dictates the prices at which dealers may sell, it will be invalidated. If it is part of a package of restraints which includes resale price maintenance, it also is likely to be invalidated.

Does this make sense? Both territorial restraints and resale price maintenance accomplish the same thing, serving to assure the dealers higher margins which allow them to pay for promotion and other competitive services. Resale price maintenance does this by eliminating intrabrand competition with respect to price, while territorial restraints can do this by foreclosing intrabrand competition entirely. Yet resale price maintenance is *per se* unlawful, while most territorial restraints are perfectly acceptable. The principal justification for this difference is that although territorial restraints may eliminate all intrabrand competition, they do not prevent each dealer from adjusting his prices in response to competition from other brands. Resale price maintenance removes that discretion from the dealers and places it entirely in the hands of the supplier, who may be tempted to collude with other suppliers in setting retail prices.

There was a time not long ago when territorial and customer restraints also were subject to *per se* illegality. Anyone responsible for marketing through dealers in the late sixties and most of the seventies will recall operating under a very strict set of rules regarding such restraints. In the 1967 case of *United States* v. *Arnold, Schwinn & Co.*, the Supreme Court indicated that it would be a *per se* violation not only for a supplier to specify the prices at which dealers may sell, but also for a supplier to limit the territories in which dealers may sell or the customers to whom they may sell. The Court held that once the dealer took title to the goods, he had to be left free to sell them as he saw fit. But *Schwinn* was overruled ten years later in the case of *Continental T.V., Inc.* v. *GTE Sylvania Inc.*, probably the most important marketing decision on the books, and that changed the rules dramatically. In *Sylvania*, the Supreme Court recognized the economic utility of territorial restraints and other sales restraints—with the one exception of resale price maintenance, which remains *per se* unlawful. Other sales restraints imposed on dealers are now upheld where reasonable, although it is important to remember that even these restraints can be unlawful in particular circumstances.

Arrangements Among Dealers.

One of these circumstances is initiation of the restraints by the dealers themselves, acting in concert with one another. Where dealers jointly conceive an arrangement to eliminate competition among them through territorial or other restraints, and force their common supplier to impose and police these restraints against his own judgment, the plan will not be upheld. Economic theorists have argued that the motivation of a *supplier* for eliminating intrabrand competition is likely to be improving the competitiveness of his brand, while the motivation of *dealers* for eliminating intrabrand competition is more likely to be nothing more than lessening competition and raising prices.

But what if the dealers' motive really is to eliminate a genuine free riding problem which the supplier has not seen fit to confront? What if the dealers convince their supplier to establish the restraints and enforce them? It may be argued that even though the dealers in these circumstances obviously would be agreeing to divide markets, the plan would be procompetitive, every bit as much as though the supplier had thought of it first. Attorneys in the Justice Department and two members of the Federal Trade Commission have argued that such an arrangement should be judged under the rule of reason and not be unlawful *per se*. So far, however, this view has not been adopted by the courts, and if the dealers turn out to be the source of the restraint, there is no guarantee that it will be upheld.

Diminished Competition.

Even if the supplier imposes non-price sales restraints unilaterally, without any price fixing or dealer coercion, these restraints still are not always found reasonable or lawful. If there is little or no competition from other brands already, there may be little need to encourage the dealers to compete against those other brands more vigorously. In such a situation competition among dealers of the same brand may be the most important form of competition there is. Similarly, if there is no free riding problem to overcome, and little danger of a free riding problem developing, there may be little reason to prevent dealers from competing with one another, and vertical restraints may simply make it easier for suppliers to conspire with one another to control the market at the dealer level. Where dealers engage in few pre-sale services, do not pay for promotions and do not perform repairs, free riding may not be a factor.

The supplier may also be engaged in some distribution himself, either by operating distributors or by selling directly to certain users. (This is sometimes referred to as "dual distribution.") If a supplier imposing territorial or customer restraints is really doing nothing more than insulating his own sales efforts from competition by his dealers, without any free riding problem being involved at all, the restraints can face tough sledding if the brand involved has a significant market share. Note, however, that suppliers who operate some of their own dealers themselves ordinarily are entitled to protect those dealers from genuine free riding incursions, just as with any other dealer.

THE JUSTICE DEPARTMENT'S GUIDELINES

The Department of Justice recently issued its "Vertical Restraints Guidelines," detailing the Department's current enforcement policy with regard to vertical restraints other than price fixing. (The full text of the Guidelines appears at the end of this volume.) The Guidelines are not binding on any court, and they do not necessarily describe the standards which the courts currently are applying. They have been subject to strong criticism in Congress for these reasons, and the National Association of Attorneys General, representing the fifty states, has adopted alternative guidelines of its own. Nevertheless, the Justice Department's Guidelines are largely consistent with the economic rationale behind most of the recent cases, and they can be expected to have an impact.

The Guidelines can be a nightmare of complexity for the uninitiated, and have been called the antitrust lawyers' answer to the Internal Revenue Code. For those hardy and curious readers who have the desire or the need to gain some basic familiarity with the Guidelines, the most prominent features are described in the pages which follow. For those who can contain their curiosity until the need arises, and would just as soon skip the next six pages,   suffice it to say that   the new Guidelines set up a relatively precise set of standards, including some highly mathematical tests, under which most non-price vertical restraints are likely to pass muster, at least at the Justice Department.

The basic approach taken in the Guidelines is built upon the proposition that where any one particular brand enjoys only a modest share of the market, it does not matter very much whether restraints are placed on the dealers who sell that brand because even if that brand's prices are driven up by the restraints, this would not have any significant effect on the overall level of prices in the market as a whole. In the long run, competitive pressure from the other brands could be expected to keep the prices of all brands at a competitive level.

Only when a large percentage of total sales in the entire market is subject to a restraint is there any real possibility for unreasonable limitations on competition, in the Department's view, and then only with regard to those suppliers who themselves control a significant share of the market. While this approach is consistent with the approach most recently taken by the courts, the Justice Department has gone a step beyond and developed a mathematical "market structure screen," to screen out cases that do not warrant further investigation.

Market Structure Screen.

The simplest test under the "screen" is based on straight market share figures. If a nonprice vertical restraint is employed by a brand having a market share of no more than 10 percent, the Justice Department will not challenge it. If the market share exceeds 10 percent, the Department will apply two other mathematical tests it has created to screen potential cases, the Vertical Restraints Index (or "VRI"), and the "coverage ratio." The VRI measures both how widely a restraint is used in an industry, and the relative size of the firms using it. The VRI at the supplier level is calculated by taking the market share of each supplier who utilizes the particular restraint under inquiry (territorial restraints, for example), squaring that market share, and adding the squares together. The VRI at the dealer level is calculated in the same way, using the market shares of the dealers who are subject to the restraint.

Under this approach, if there are four suppliers in a market, each one has a market share of 25 percent, and all of them impose territorial restraints, the VRI for territorial restraints at the supplier level will be 2,500 ($25^2 + 25^2 + 25^2 + 25^2 = 625 + 625 + 625 + 625 = 2,500$). If there are ten dealers in the market, but only two of them are subject to territorial restraints, and the shares of those two are 5 percent and 20 percent, the VRI for territorial restraints at the dealer level will be 425 ($5^2 + 20^2 = 25 + 400 = 425$).

The "coverage ratio" is simply the share of the overall relevant market which is subject to the particular restraint. For example, if five dealers having a combined market share of 50 percent are subject to territorial restraints, the coverage ratio for that restraint at the dealer level is 50 percent. The principal difference between the VRI and the coverage ratio is that the VRI reflects both the size of the firms using the restraint in the market and how widely the restraint is used as an overall percentage of the market, while the coverage ratio reflects only the latter.

Four Tests.

The Guidelines set up four tests for screening out cases in which the potential effect on the market is so small that the restraint will be presumed lawful:

1. As already noted, if the firm employing the restraint has a market share of 10 percent or less, the restraint will not be challenged.

2. If the VRI is under 1,200 and the coverage ratio is under 60 percent at the *same* level (either the supplier level or the dealer level), the restraint will not be challenged. The theory

here is that there must be both a VRI above 1,200 at the level at which the restraint was instigated, *and* a coverage ratio above 60 percent at the other level, in order for there to be a possibility of an anticompetitive effect. If *neither* of these thresholds is met at *either* of the two levels, this test cannot be met.

3. If the VRI is under 1,200 at both levels, the restraint will not be challenged.

4. If the coverage ratio is below 60 percent at both levels, the restraint will not be challenged.

As points of reference, it is useful to note that a VRI of 1,200 is equivalent to use of a restraint by either one firm with a 34.6 percent market share, two firms with 24.5 percent shares each, three firms with 20 percent each, or seven firms with 13 percent each.

Note that in computing the coverage ratio, the Guidelines indicate that for purposes of restraints such as customer and territorial restraints—where there is a risk that the restraints will facilitate collusion among suppliers or among dealers—current market share is the significant consideration. In the case of restraints such as exclusive dealing, on the other hand, where exclusion of competitors is the primary risk, capacity is more important than current market share. Since these distinctions are often difficult to make, the Guidelines employ a rule of thumb that whichever figure (market share or capacity) produces the larger coverage ratio, that figure should be used. And in the case of retailers, the number of outlets may be used as a substitute for capacity levels where data on capacity is not available.

Note that in making the calculations, any vertically integrated firms (e.g., suppliers who own their own dealers) will be included in the relevant market and will be assumed to be employing the restraint at issue. Dual distributors (e.g., suppliers who own some but not all of their dealers) will be included as well, and will also be assumed to use the restraint to the extent that they are selling through their own outlets.

Examples.

The Guidelines give four examples of how the screen mechanism will be applied:

Example One. Two suppliers with 8 percent market shares and two dealers with 9 percent market shares employ vertical restraints. Applying the first test, the Department will not challenge the use of vertical restraints by these firms.

Example Two. Two suppliers with 20 percent market shares and one supplier with a 10 percent market share employ territorial and customer restrictions. The supplier market VRI $= 20^2 + 20^2 + 10^2 = 400 + 400 + 100 = 900$. Fifty percent of the supplier market is subject to restraint. Applying the second test, the Department will not challenge these vertical restraints.

Example Three. Five suppliers with 15 percent market shares and three dealers with 19 percent market shares are subject to territorial and customer restrictions. The dealer level VRI $= 19^2 + 19^2 + 19^2 = 361 + 361 + 361 = 1,083$. The supplier level VRI $= 15^2 + 15^2 + 15^2 + 15^2 + 15^2 = 225 + 225 + 225 + 225 + 225 = 1,125$. Applying the third test, the Department will not further scrutinize these restraints.

Example Four. Fifty percent of the supplier market and 55 percent of the capacity in the dealer market are subject to exclusive dealing restrictions. Applying the fourth test, the Department will not further scrutinize these restraints.

Restraints Not Screened Out.

If the restraint under scrutiny is of large enough dimension to get through the screen, the Justice Department will not automatically presume that it is unlawful, but will go on to examine other factors under a "structured" rule of reason analysis, to determine whether enforcement action is warranted. First, the Department will look at "ease of entry," placing more emphasis on this single factor than most courts previously have. In the Department's view, vertical restraints normally pose little threat to competition if it is relatively easy for new suppliers and dealers to enter the same market. (Hint: You can be a hero by setting up an "Ease of Entry" file in your office now to keep press clippings on companies entering the industry, and having the file ready if the need arises.)

If entry appears to be more difficult at the level where the restraint is of concern, the Department will proceed to consider any history of actual anticompetitive effects caused by the restraint. If there is no history to examine because the restraint is too new, or if the historical information is inconclusive, the Department will go on to examine other factors, including: (1) just how high the market shares of the firms employing the restraint actually are; (2) how likely it is that the restraint can be used to facilitate collusion among suppliers of different brands or among the dealers; (3) how exclusionary the restraint will be to would-be rivals; (4) the intent of the firms using the restraint, if there is evidence of intent; and (5) whether even small firms or firms just entering the market use the restraint (a sign that the restraint is probably efficient).

The Department also will consider whether there are valid procompetitive efficiencies associated with the restraint, such as elimination of a free rider problem and encouragement of new entry, although "an inability to demonstrate efficiencies should not be interpreted as proof of an anticompetitive explanation for a restraint." In fact, the Department points out that "the reason that a particular restraint is successful in increasing consumer welfare may not be clear until long after the restraint is first used," and businesses should not be deterred from experimenting with vertical restraints simply because the "benefits are unclear."

Limitations.

It is important to recognize that the Guidelines have certain limitations. First, they are only a statement of the Justice Department's enforcement intentions. As noted earlier, they are not binding on any court, and do not necessarily set forth the standards which would be applied by a court in cases instituted by private parties. This qualification is significant, because most vertical restraint cases are, in fact, brought by private litigants.

Second, the Guidelines may be of limited utility for some companies deciding whether or not to impose vertical restraints because the VRI and capacity ratio cannot be calculated without knowing how broad the market is, which suppliers and dealers in the market already utilize the restraint, and approximately what each of their market shares and capacities are. Some "markets" are easier to define than others in terms of which products compete in the same market, and in terms of how broad the market is geographically. But even if there is relative certainty over the parameters of the market, it may be difficult to learn whether others use the same restraint, and even more difficult to learn what their market shares and capacities are.

While the Justice Department can obtain this type of information in most cases, using its investigatory powers, private corporations often have no way of gathering reliable data of this kind. Without the data, the VRI and coverage ratio are of only theoretical interest. In some industries, of course, data on sales are collected by market research organizations and published. Trade associations sometimes collect data of this kind as well. And if the dealers are retailers, the Guidelines permit the use of figures on the number of retailers using the restraint as a substitute for market share statistics.

For practical purposes, the clearest area of comfort in the Guidelines is likely to be found in the low market share proviso. So long as a firm knows that its own market share is 10 percent or less, it can expect to enjoy a pretty secure "safe harbor," at least with respect to the Justice Department.

When all is said and done, the bottom line for assessing nonprice sales restraints—with or without reference to the Guidelines—is that if the supplier has sound marketing reasons for establishing the restraints in the first place, or has an insignificant market share, the restraints usually will be upheld. If the restraints were forced upon the supplier by the dealers against the supplier's own judgment, or if the supplier's motive was simply to stifle competition, the restraints are more likely

to be struck down as unreasonable—and resale price maintenance almost always will be illegal.

Permissible Restraints.

So much for determining illegality. The majority of sales
restraints are lawful, and the remainder of this chapter will address them all. What limitations is a supplier permitted to impose on his dealers, and what limitations are not allowed?

Territorial Restraints.

A simple territorial restraint prohibits a dealer from making
sales outside of a defined geographic territory. It forbids the
dealer from opening outlets outside the territory, sending his
trucks outside the territory, sending sales representatives outside the territory or delivering to customers outside the territory
by any other means.

Simple territorial restraints have been upheld in a number
of cases where the purpose of the restraint was to eliminate free
riding or the potential for free riding. These restraints are commonly imposed on distributors of beer, newspapers and a variety of other products. If dealers are not permitted to make
sales outside their own territories, they will find it difficult, if
not impossible, to take a free ride on the efforts of neighboring
dealers. The legality of territorial restraints has come into question primarily in cases where the principal reason for imposing
the restraint allegedly was not to eliminate free riding, but to
eliminate competition—between dealers and the supplier or
among the dealers themselves—and to raise prices in the market as a whole.

A simple territorial restraint can be agreed upon with language such as that which appears in **Sample Provision 1**. Of
course, lawyers always have to tailor contract language to fit the
precise requirements of each individual situation, but sample
provisions are provided in this volume as a general guide to the
basic kinds of restrictions and obligations that are permissible

SAMPLE PROVISION 1
SIMPLE TERRITORIAL RESTRAINT

Dealer may sell the product only within the territory defined in Exhibit A.*

---

*"Exhibit A" should provide a detailed description of the territorial boundaries.

---

under the law. Marketing executives should be cognizant of what they can ask for and what goes too far. Naturally, these sample clauses should never just be lifted verbatim to draft "do-it-yourself" contracts on the backs of napkins. But a reading of these sample provisions can serve as a checklist of the most important types of arrangements that can be included in a marketing program, to be sure that nothing is overlooked.

Multi-Tier Territorial Restraints.

For practical purposes, the pro-competitive effects of territorial restraints—specifically, the elimination of "free riding"—may not be achievable by a simple territorial restraint such as the one discussed immediately above. Even if a dealer sells only within his own territory, his customers may "transship" into adjacent territories and resell there, resulting in the same free rider effect which the territorial restraint was intended to eliminate.

To combat this problem, some suppliers have imposed "multi-tier" territorial restraints, which not only require dealers to limit their own sales to their territory, but also require them to sell only to customers who also will limit *their* sales to the same territory. To name but two examples, Amana has imposed this kind of restraint on its microwave oven dealers and Royal Crown Cola has imposed one on its soft drink bottlers. Both

SAMPLE PROVISION 2
MULTI-TIER TERRITORIAL RESTRAINT

Dealer may sell the product only for ultimate resale to consumers within the territory defined in Exhibit A.*

---

*"Exhibit A" should provide a detailed description of the territory.

---

have litigated the legality of these restraints successfully. Of course, dealers may not always realize that some of their customers are transshipping until after the problem has surfaced, at which point the dealer is obligated to convince the customer to discontinue the practice, or stop selling to that customer altogether. A multi-tier territorial restraint may be imposed with language such as that in **Sample Provision 2.**

In one respect, this type of restraint may be characterized as a "customer restraint" because it limits the dealer to selling only to customers who will not resell outside of the territory. Where feasible, the same goal sometimes may be achieved with a straightforward customer restraint limiting the dealer to selling only to end-users, who are not expected to resell the product at all. Courts have upheld multi-tier territorial restraints in a number of cases, and, in the soft drink industry, the federal Soft Drink Interbrand Competition Act of 1980 specifically recognizes the legality of this kind of restraint in most circumstances.

Customer Restraints.

Customer restraints prohibit dealers from selling to certain classes of customers, usually because the supplier has decided that particular types of customers should be served through other channels. The restraint may be phrased affirmatively to require the dealer to sell only to particular classes of customers, or it may be phrased negatively to prohibit the dealer from selling to certain classes of customers, such as original equipment manufacturers, governmental units or overseas customers. Typically the supplier has chosen to serve these customers directly, or to reserve them for more specialized dealers.

To cite some examples, wholesale distributors of certain brands of appliances, bicycles and sporting goods have been restricted to selling only to retailers who have been authorized to carry the line by the manufacturer. Wholesalers of certain brands of drug products and heavy equipment have been prohibited by the manufacturer from pursuing export sales. Customer restraints may be agreed upon in a number of forms, including those which appear in **Sample Provision 3.**

The rationale behind these restraints is that dealers will engage in more effective competition against other brands if they

SAMPLE PROVISION 3
CUSTOMER RESTRAINTS

1. Wholesaler may sell the product only to retailers authorized by Supplier.
   OR
2. Retailer may sell the product only to customers who [use] [consume] the product themselves, and not to resell it.
   OR
3. Retailer may not sell the product to customers for resale.
   OR
4. Dealer may not sell the product to any government body or government-operated enterprise; to any "original equipment manufacturer"; to any customer located outside the United States; or to any "national account." "Original equipment manufacturer" shall mean a customer which incorporates the product as a component of a product which it sells.

are required to focus their efforts on particular categories of customers, rather than scattering their efforts and trying to "skim the cream" in every category. Also, by limiting wholesalers to selling only to "authorized" retailers, suppliers can protect against free riding at the retail level. Customer restraints have been upheld in a number of cases, and courts have permitted suppliers to terminate dealers who sold to unapproved retailers.

A few courts have been wary, however, that particular customer restraints may be nothing but a ploy to eliminate sales to discounters, and thereby maintain resale prices. If there is evidence proving that the supplier's reason for imposing a customer restraint was not to promote interbrand competition at all, but simply to prevent discounting or otherwise to restrain competition, the restriction is more likely to be found unlawful.

Of course, it may be difficult in certain cases for a dealer to know in advance that a customer intends to resell the product rather than consume it himself, and as with any "transshipper," he may have to be permitted one bite at the apple. If the dealer knowingly permits the situation to persist, however, he may be risking termination himself.

Location Clauses.

In some situations, particularly at the retail level, most dealers sell from fixed locations. Customers visit them, but they do not call upon customers. In these situations it is not uncommon for suppliers to impose location clauses, limiting each dealer to selling only from one or more designated locations. This is generally not considered as severe a restriction as a territorial restriction (although it is sometimes characterized as a species of territorial restriction). Unlike an outright territorial restraint, a location clause does not actually prohibit the dealer from soliciting or making sales to distant customers, if his business lends itself to such an approach.

In certain circumstances, however, a location clause can be just as effective as an outright territorial restraint in limiting intrabrand competition. Where sales must be made on the dealer's premises because of the nature of the product, or where customers are not likely to travel far in search of the product, a location clause will have the practical effect of eliminating virtually all competition among dealers of the same brand. For example, if a brand of washing machines were sold by only one dealer in each major metropolitan area, the distances involved would foreclose the development of much intrabrand competition. If there were four dealers in each area instead, intrabrand competition would soon develop. But if the product were fast food, substantial intrabrand competition among the four dealers in the area would not be as likely to materialize, because the product is perishable and is normally consumed on the premises. Also, most consumers are not as likely to travel any appreciable distance to comparison-shop for such inexpensive items as hamburgers, to find out which outlet of the same chain has the lowest price.

Location clauses consistently have been upheld in numerous cases, even during the years when outright territorial restraints were considered *per se* illegal under the *Schwinn* decision. Many of the cases have involved the automobile industry and the television industry, where location clauses have been quite common. A location clause can be agreed upon with language such as that in **Sample Provision 4.**

SAMPLE PROVISION 4
LOCATION CLAUSE

Dealer may sell the product only from the location or locations described in Exhibit A [unless otherwise authorized by Supplier in writing].*

---

*"Exhibit A" should list the precise address of each authorized location.

Areas of Primary Responsibility.

Sometimes a supplier determines that he does not want to prevent his dealers from competing with one another, yet he does want to insure that each dealer will maintain adequate service and promotional efforts within that dealer's own area. In an attempt to have his cake and eat it too, the supplier may try imposing "areas of primary responsibility," within which each dealer is responsible for maintaining adequate distribution and service, without being prevented from selling in other areas. But these arrangements are often difficult to enforce. Also, they may place a heavy burden on those dealers who face steady "invasions" from neighboring dealers of the same brand, since the "invaded" dealers must continue to devote the required time and money even if other dealers are "skimming the cream" of their best customers. If the invaded dealer cannot meet his service obligations and still earn a profit, this kind of arrangement will not survive. Area of primary responsibility clauses have been upheld in a number of cases, although dealers sometimes have complained that they operate as *de facto* territorial restraints.

An area of primary responsibility can be arranged with language like that in **Sample Provision 5.** Primary responsibility clauses also can be more specific than this in detailing the min-

SAMPLE PROVISION 5
AREA OF PRIMARY RESPONSIBILITY CLAUSE

Dealer's Area of Primary Responsibility is described in Exhibit A hereto. Dealer will devote its primary efforts within that Area, and, although Dealer may also sell outside that Area, it will at all times devote sufficient efforts and funds within the Area to satisfy Supplier that it can and will maximize sales of the product within the Area.

SAMPLE PROVISION 6
BEST EFFORTS CLAUSE

---

1. Dealer will use its best efforts to maximize sales of the Product. Dealer will call upon every [potential] [authorized] customer [in its territory] [in its area of primary responsibility] with sufficient frequency to maximize sales of the Product.

OR

2. Dealer shall devote its best efforts to the sale and promotion of sales of the Product [within the territory] so as to achieve maximum distribution and sales for the Product [within the territory].

---

imum level of effort required of each dealer within his own territory. If the supplier expects particular types of efforts to be made or particular levels of promotional activity, these can be spelled out.

Best Efforts Clauses.

A "best efforts" clause is not, strictly speaking, a restraint, but it can be employed to achieve some of the same objectives of an area of primary responsibility provision. By undertaking to devote his best efforts to marketing the supplier's product, the dealer gives his assurance that he will promote and service the product to the fullest extent of his capabilities, and the supplier is afforded the right to terminate the dealer for failing to fulfill this promise (subject, of course, to any special state or federal termination legislation). A best efforts obligation can be agreed to with language such as that in **Sample Provision 6.**

Since the principal shortcoming of best efforts clauses is the difficulty of measuring performance, it can be useful to include specific criteria. These may include specification of how many employees the dealer will devote to the line, or how many trucks or advertising dollars. Alternatively, the clause may spell out which types of potential customers must be called on, or how much coverage must be achieved. Of course, if it is clear that a dealer is devoting greater effort to other lines, he obviously is not devoting his "best" efforts to the line imposing the clause. Beyond that, assessing compliance with best efforts clauses can be a very subjective and uncertain matter, particularly if specific criteria are not enumerated.

Profit Pass-Overs.

A profit pass-over is a device which enjoyed greater popularity during the decade when territorial restraints were considered *per se* unlawful under the *Schwinn* case. It involves a promise by each dealer to turn over a specified part of his profits on sales outside his territory to those dealers who have primary responsibility for promotion and service in the areas where those sales are made. An example appears in **Sample Provision 7.**

SAMPLE PROVISION 7
PROFIT PASS-OVER

If Dealer makes sales to customers located within the Area of Primary Responsibility of another dealer, Dealer will pay a Brand Development Fee to compensate that other dealer for the expense of promoting the product within that Area and maintaining facilities there. The Brand Development Fee will be _____ percent of the selling price. The Fee will be paid to the Supplier, which will administer all Brand Development Fees and will forward payment to the appropriate Dealer in each case, in accordance with procedures which the Supplier will specify from time to time.

Profit pass-overs have been subject to criticism in the past because if they were set too high, they would remove all incentive for a dealer to sell outside of his territory, and might really function as a territorial restraint, which, during the *Schwinn* era, was *per se* illegal. If territorial separation is desired, and if this is a reasonable objective given the particular circumstances, this can be achieved more directly at the present time with territorial restraints, most of which should now be lawful. For this reason, profit pass-overs are no longer particularly desirable for most companies, except where territorial restrictions are also in place and the profit pass-over is employed simply as a means of rectifying the effects of unauthorized "invasions" by one dealer into another dealer's territory.

Sales Quotas.

Another means for encouraging dealers to promote a product is to impose sales quotas, and to terminate dealers who fail to meet them. Sales quotas must be realistic, of course, or practically every dealer will face termination. They also must be administered and enforced fairly. In addition, it should be recognized that dealers may be unable, or simply unwilling, to meet sales goals unless they are afforded some measure of insulation from the "free riding" of neighboring dealers. This may require the imposition of territorial restraints or other limitations.

Sales quotas, in the absence of other restraints, allow the dealers the greatest freedom of operation. They require each dealer to sell a certain volume, but place no limits on where, how or to whom these sales may be made. A sales quota may be agreed upon using language such as that in **Sample Provision 8.**

A potential problem with quotas, it should be recognized, may be the encouragement of discounting. Some of the dealers may begin cutting prices in an effort to meet their quotas.

SAMPLE PROVISION 8
SALES QUOTA

Dealer will sell at least ____ units each [year] [month] during the term of this Agreement.

Resale Prices.

At this writing, resale price maintenance remains *per se* unlawful. As recently as 1980, Cuisinarts paid a $250,000 fine for resale price maintenance in a criminal antitrust case brought during the Carter Administration. Under the Reagan Administration, however, the Department of Justice has assumed a more tolerant approach, dismissing on its own a resale price maintenance case which had earlier been instituted against Mack Trucks. The Department has argued in the Supreme Court and elsewhere that resale price maintenance should be subject to the rule of reason and should be upheld in some circumstances, particularly where it is merely a subsidiary feature of another restraint. For example, if a dealer is totally prohibited from selling outside of his territory, we have seen that this is usually reasonable; if he is instead permitted to make sales outside the territory but only at a fixed price, that may be reasonable too, so long as he remains free to set any price he wants within his territory, and there are other brands competing in the market. To date, the Reagan Administration has never filed a suit challenging resale price maintenance, but private actions are still brought, and courts still consider the practice illegal.

In any event, merely *suggesting* resale prices has always been lawful, provided there genuinely is nothing more than a suggestion, without any agreement on the part of dealers to adhere to particular prices. Suggesting resale prices, and other lawful measures for influencing resale prices, are discussed in detail in Chapter Five.

Given the present situation, a supplier simply may choose

SAMPLE PROVISION 9
PRICING CLAUSE

Dealer may sell the Product at whatever price it chooses, in Dealer's sole discretion. Supplier may, from time to time, suggest prices at which Dealer might sell, but such suggestions are not binding upon Dealer.

---

to remain silent on the subject of price in his distribution agreements. On the other hand, he may wish affirmatively to disclaim any intent to maintain resale prices, particularly if he makes a practice of suggesting resale prices.

A price clause incorporating these considerations can be phrased like the one in **Sample Provision 9.** If a supplier employs a clause such as this, he must, of course, be careful not to coerce dealers into agreeing to adhere to the suggested prices.

Consignment Price Clauses.

Where a dealer carries a supplier's products on consignment, the supplier is entitled to decide on the prices at which those products will be sold. The consignment must be legitimate, however, because if it is found to be a sham, the pricing arrangement likely will be considered unlawful. Where the supplier retains title and control over his products, as evidenced by such indicators as retention of risk of loss, the supplier's right to determine prices will be recognized. Where the arrangement is labeled a "consignment," but the dealer really bears the risk of loss, such pricing control will not be permitted. There is no single touchstone for distinguishing "true" consignments from "sham" consignments, and the courts generally look to all of the facts and circumstances of each case, including the language of the contract, who pays for the freight, and who maintains the insurance.

SAMPLE PROVISION 10
CONSIGNMENT PRICING CLAUSE

> Dealer will sell those quantities of the Product which Supplier provides to it on consignment only at prices specified by Supplier.

A price clause in a consignment arrangement can be agreed upon with language such as that in **Sample Provision 10**. The supplier can order his dealers to raise or lower the prices of inventory items held on consignment at any time, or can print his prices on the packages if he chooses. The supplier calls the tune, but he also has paid the piper by financing the dealer's inventory.

Appearance of Facility and Personnel Clause.

As discussed earlier, suppliers sometimes find themselves facing litigation because they cut off sales of their products to shabby-looking discount houses. Frequently, discounters are able to charge low prices precisely because they provide few amenities and therefore operate with low overhead. The supplier may not care about the prices being charged by these establishments, but only about their appearance and their failure to provide adequate displays, sales assistance and service. Yet, following such a cut-off, the supplier may be charged with having terminated the discounter for the purpose of maintaining resale prices.

One way to help establish that price was not the reason for the cut-off is to spell out appearance and performance requirements in the distribution agreement (or unilateral policy statement) and clearly base the termination upon failure to meet these requirements. An example appears in **Sample Provision 11.** More detailed requirements can be included in an operating

SAMPLE PROVISION 11
APPEARANCE CLAUSE

Dealer shall maintain its place of business in an attractive, orderly and sanitary condition satisfactory to Supplier and in conformance with all applicable governmental codes and regulations.

Dealer shall display and demonstrate the Products in a manner and to an extent satisfactory to Supplier and shall maintain an adequate stock of inventory and adequate facilities for the storage, handling, sale and service thereof.

Dealer shall employ sufficient personnel to demonstrate, sell and service the Products to Supplier's satisfaction, and shall train these personnel in the demonstration, use, sales and service of the Products in a manner satisfactory to Supplier.

Dealer shall comply with the requirements of Supplier's Operating Manual, which may be amended from time to time in Supplier's sole discretion.

manual, right down to the quality of the floor coverings and the number of towels in the bathrooms. Of course, if the evidence shows that the supplier's real reason for a termination was indeed price fixing, provisions of this kind cannot be expected to make a difference. Where evidence of the supplier's purpose is ambiguous, however, a clause of this kind can help to demonstrate the true nature of the supplier's objectives.

This type of clause, alone or together with other sales restrictions, can go a long way toward insuring that products are sold to consumers in an atmosphere which fits the supplier's marketing concept. So long as the supplier's objectives are legitimate, considerable control over the dealers' facilities and sales techniques can be achieved. In various combinations, sales restraints can give the supplier real influence, enabling him to shape the way in which his products are presented and sold to the public.

RESTRICTING DEALERS' PURCHASES

Not all vertical restraints which are imposed upon dealers restrict selling. Dealers also can be restricted in what they may purchase. Purchasing restrictions include "exclusive dealing" arrangements, "requirements" contracts, "tying" provisions and "full line forcing." Exclusive dealing and requirements contracts have been upheld in numerous cases over the years, although not without exception. Tying and full line forcing have fared less well in the courts, with tying being subjected to *per se* illegality in certain cases. Unlike the sales restraints we just finished discussing, which limit what dealers may do with the supplier's products, purchasing restrictions have an impact on what the dealers may do with the products of *other* suppliers. This effect has required the courts to judge these restraints using a somewhat different analysis.

Exclusive Dealing Clauses.

Exclusive dealing is a restriction which is imposed by a supplier on a customer, forbidding the customer from purchasing some type of product from any other supplier: "If you want to buy widgets from me, you may not buy them from anyone else." Although the legal treatment of exclusive dealing has had a roller coaster history, during the past twenty years these arrangements generally have been upheld so long as other suppliers are not foreclosed from reaching the ultimate market and competition is not unreasonably limited. An example of an exclusive dealing clause appears in **Sample Provision 12.**

Exclusive dealing can serve to intensify interbrand competition (among different brands) by forcing each distributor to concentrate his efforts on a single brand, eliminating the prob-

SAMPLE PROVISION 12
EXCLUSIVE DEALING CLAUSE

> Dealer will not sell or offer to sell any [widgets] other than those purchased from Supplier.

lem of divided loyalties. This effect was illustrated in a case in which Royal Crown Cola was upheld in its effort to block an attempt by one of its bottlers to begin carrying a second brand of cola. The court pointed out that this would put the bottler in the position to decide which brand to promote when, for how long, and by how much. Exclusive dealing has also been common in the distribution of hearing aids, farm machinery and heavy construction equipment. A dealer who carries only one brand of a product necessarily becomes a devoted advocate of that brand, providing more vigorous competition against other brands. Also, the supplier himself will be more willing to assist his dealers to compete, by providing training, financing and equipment, if the dealers are not dividing their efforts among many brands.

The principal concern which exclusive dealing may raise is foreclosure of rival suppliers. The danger is that if too many dealers in an industry become bound to exclusive dealing arrangements, some suppliers, particularly newcomers, may have no viable way to reach consumers and may find themselves foreclosed from the market almost entirely. In such cases exclusive dealing may be struck down under the rule of reason for doing competition more harm than good.

Exclusive Dealing Under the Guidelines.

The Justice Department's "Vertical Restraints Guidelines" address exclusive dealing, and apply the same "market structure screen" that was described earlier. If an exclusive dealing clause is not presumed lawful under the "screen" on the ground that the market shares involved are too small or the extent of exclusive dealing in the market as a whole is not very extensive, the Department will proceed to examine other factors, principally "ease of entry" and the "exclusionary effect" of the exclusive arrangement. The Justice Department's approach is consistent with the standards which have been applied by the courts in recent years, but it is more precise due to the addition of the Department's screening device.

Exclusive dealing is subject to two special rules under the Guidelines, which distinguish it from territorial and customer restraints. First, in computing the "coverage ratio" for purposes of making a rule of reason analysis, capacity figures are supposed to be used rather than sales figures. Data on capacity will be more meaningful than historical sales data, since the degree of foreclosure brought about by exclusive dealing depends upon how much additional capacity will remain for others, whether or not it is already in use. Second, "ease of entry" for purposes of exclusive dealing should always be measured in the market which is being partially foreclosed, and if entry is "very easy" there, the Department will presume that the exclusive dealing is lawful.

As a further guide, the authors of the Guidelines presume that exclusive dealing arrangements between suppliers and dealers are not likely to foreclose new suppliers from the market, even when imposed by a relatively large supplier, if the arrangement is limited to one year and does not penalize dealers who subsequently switch to other suppliers. An exclusionary effect is considered more likely where large suppliers impose exclusive dealing contracts with long terms and with "major financial penalties" against dealers for switching suppliers.

Exclusive dealing should not be confused with "exclusive distributorships," the term applied to arrangements in which a supplier promises not to appoint more than one dealer in each territory. Unfortunately, the Justice Department Guidelines invite confusion over this terminology by defining both exclusive distributorships and traditional exclusive dealing at one point as "exclusive dealing arrangements." You can distinguish between the two by remembering that exclusive dealing restricts the dealer, while exclusive distributorships restrict the supplier.

Requirements Contracts.

A "requirements contract" is a variation of exclusive dealing by which a customer promises to purchase all or a specified part of his requirements of a product from a particular supplier, and the supplier agrees to fill those requirements. As with other exclusive dealing arrangements, requirements contracts have been upheld where competition is not unreasonably foreclosed in the market. A requirements provision can be agreed to with language such as that in **Sample Provision 13.**

SAMPLE PROVISION 13
REQUIREMENTS CLAUSE

Customer will purchase all of its requirements of fool's gold from Supplier for a period of _____ years, and Supplier will supply such requirements.

Tie-Ins.

Sellers lucky enough to have popular products may be faced with enticing opportunities to convince their customers to purchase other, less attractive products from them as well. For example, if a supplier's sales representative is calling on a dealer to sell a "hot" line of electronic typewriters, this may present an excellent opportunity to sell that dealer on carrying some of his typewriter ribbons too, even though the ribbons may be less unique and desirable. There is nothing unlawful about using the appeal of a particularly attractive product to get a foot in the door and then try to sell other, less popular items as well.

If, however, dealers or other customers are actually forced to purchase items they do not want in order to obtain the products they do want, this becomes "tying." The sought after product is known as the "tying product" and the unwanted item is termed the "tied product." Some tying agreements have been classified as *per se* unlawful, but so many exceptions and prerequisites to the *per se* rule have developed over the years that tying sometimes has been referred to as a "soft-core" *per se* offense, to distinguish it from such "hard-core" offenses as price fixing.

If our fictional typewriter supplier had substantial market power in the electronic typewriter market and were to tell dealers, "To get my fast-moving typewriter you also have to take an equivalent amount of my mediocre ribbons," this would constitute a tie-in. The supplier's market power in the "tying" product's market could be a function of a large market share, a unique product which other suppliers cannot duplicate, or the protection of a significant patent. If the hypothetical tie-in were imposed, other suppliers of ribbons—the "tied" product— would suffer, because a certain volume of business would be foreclosed for which they otherwise could have competed. The dealers involved would suffer because they would be forced to purchase ribbons they did not really want. In situations like this, some courts have concluded that the arrangement warrants condemnation. But some tie-ins make a lot of sense and result in real efficiencies. Tying cases can be difficult, as illustrated by the story of Data General.

CASE HISTORY: A Hard Sell for Hardware.

Data General Corporation, the computer manufacturer, developed a highly-regarded operating system a few years ago known as "RDOS," which could be used with its "NOVA" computer system. As part of the system, it also marketed a NOVA central processing unit, or "CPU," on which the RDOS software could be run.

Data General's policy was to license the RDOS system only to customers who also purchased its NOVA CPU. To accomplish this, it made the RDOS software available only under license agreements which prohibited use of the software with any CPU which was not authorized by Data General, and the only available CPU it ever authorized was its own.

Many users in the industry considered the RDOS system to be the best of its kind—the fastest, the most comprehensive, the most widely compatible and the most field-proven. The system was copyrighted, of course, and could not be reproduced by others without utilizing information that Data General considered to be a trade secret. Because of this, RDOS had certain advantages that other software producers could not readily duplicate.

The principal purchasers of the NOVA system over the years were manufacturers of complete computer systems, designed to perform a variety of tasks. Each of these manufacturers had developed so-called "application software" which was specifically designed to accomplish these tasks, but which had to be combined with an operating system such as RDOS in order to function. Each set of application software is designed to work together with one specific operating system, however, so once a manufacturer had developed application software to function with the RDOS operating system, it was effectively "locked in" to using RDOS from that time on. Of course, this meant that for each complete system it assembled, it had to purchase the CPU from Data General because of the license restriction. The only way out was to rewrite the application software completely, to make it compatible with a different operating system, but this was prohibitively expensive. Application software can cost millions of dollars to develop, and once it is completed, its developer will stick with it because it can be used to produce any number of additional complete systems for sale to end-users.

When questioned on the subject, one manufacturer of complete systems recalled, "Economically I was in a position where I had to use RDOS. I had no choice at that point." Another observed, "It would simply take too long to change all the software that we have. We can't shut down the operation we have going." A third remarked that "it would just take forever."

Data General, for its part, believed that it had to "bundle" its software together with its CPU in order to recover its enormous investment in software research and development. Its management thought that it would be unfair to permit other CPU suppliers to reap the benefits of Data General's expensive efforts in software research. One Data General manager, however, penned a somewhat revealing internal memo suggesting that the real purpose of bundling was as much to insulate Data General's CPU from competition as to recover start up costs for the software. He wrote, "Protection from knock-off products still lies in software licensing restrictions."

The bundling requirement did not sit very well with other suppliers of CPUs, who were in competition with Data General. Other suppliers produced so-called "emulator" CPUs, which were designed to perform the same functions as Data General's NOVA CPU, and these emulator CPUs could be made compatible with the RDOS software. Early on, one of these other suppliers asked Data General for permission to use the RDOS system with its CPU, but was turned down, and this prompted Data General's decision to begin bundling. The other suppliers felt that they were being foreclosed from competing for a significant slice of the market by Data General's restrictions, leading to a lawsuit which raised these questions:

1. Were the NOVA CPU and the RDOS operating system software separate products capable of being "tied" together?

2. Did Data General possess substantial market power in any meaningful market? Would it make any difference if the RDOS software were less desirable among users? Should it matter whether the system was copyrighted? What if the RDOS software were totally unique and genuinely indispensable?

3. The manufacturers of the complete computer systems who purchased the NOVA software and CPUs knew from the beginning that they would be required to take Data General's CPUs in order to get the RDOS software, and they could have avoided this by writing their application software for other (albeit less popular) operating software at the outset. Should this make a difference? Were the other suppliers of CPUs unreasonably foreclosed from a significant portion of the market?

Tying cases can be very complicated, particularly where highly technical products are involved. Courts are often asked to determine whether the tying product is unique and whether an equivalent product can be offered by other suppliers. This may be an issue on which even experts will disagree. The court must also determine whether purchasers really were forced to buy both products, and to what extent competitors were being foreclosed. Situations such as the Data General example can only be assessed on the basis of detailed information involving the uniqueness of the product, the nature of any forcing of the purchases, and the degree of foreclosure of competitors. At this writing the Data General case has not been finally resolved, but it is useful to keep the facts of the case in mind in examining the standards which the courts apply to tie-ins generally.

When Is a Tie-In Illegal?

Tying is not always illegal, and not every arrangement that appears to be tying actually is. The standards are growing somewhat more permissive than in the past, but the rules are still very tricky, and these waters should not be navigated without a legal pilot.

To constitute a tie-in the sale of one product must actually be conditioned on the purchase of another product. The two products must be functionally distinct from one another (not a left shoe and a right shoe, for example), and there must be enough separate demand for each product alone to make it efficient to offer it for sale independently. The tie-in will be considered illegal if purchasers are forced to buy the tied product, which they did not want, because of the seller's market power over the tying product, which they did want. The tie-in will be illegal *per se* (that is, without the need for a court to consider any justifications) if there is proof that the seller's market power derives from either a high market share, a patent or similar monopoly, or a truly unique product which other sellers are not in a position to offer. If none of these elements is present, the tie-in can still be found illegal, but only if there is proof of an unreasonably adverse effect on competition.

In order to recover damages, the buyer also must be able to prove that he was injured by having to buy the tied product, which is not always possible where the tied product itself is something the buyer needed anyway, and is a good value. Competing sellers who sue are in a different posture, and must be able to show that they were prevented from making sales they otherwise would have made to a customer who was forced to buy the tied product instead of their product.

Even where all of the elements of a tie-in can be established, there are still several justifications which may be recognized. Sometimes, technological limitations require that only custom-designed inputs or accessories be used with a particular product in order to prevent breakdowns and protect the seller's reputation. For example, if our hypothetical typewriter for some reason could run satisfactorily only with the supplier's own ribbons, the supplier would be permitted to require his customers to purchase the ribbons from him too. He would even be allowed to package the two together. But this must be a legitimate necessity—the supplier cannot intentionally design the typewriter to reject other ribbons for the specific purpose of excluding competitors' ribbons. And it usually must be impossible for the supplier simply to release specifications which would enable other suppliers to produce compatible ribbons. This defense is particularly compelling in the case of new companies, which cannot afford to risk the reputations of their products by permitting them to be used in connection with other items which might cause the products to fail. In fact, newcomers may be permitted to impose a tie-in for some time even though they theoretically could release specifications for substitute products, in order to make sure that their new products get off the ground without the risk of imperilling their goodwill.

Franchising and Tying.

The law of tying took a new twist in the 1970s in connection with the then-emerging practice of franchising. In a series of cases, courts held that in the context of a franchising arrangement, the franchise itself (usually including the right to use the franchisor's trademark) could be considered a "tying product," and any items which franchisees were required to purchase from the franchisor could be considered "tied products." For example, a franchise to operate a fast-food restaurant could be treated as the sought-after tying product, while paper cups, napkins and any food items which franchisees were required to purchase from the franchisor could be considered the unwanted tied products. Again, the theory was that the franchisees were being required to buy items they did not want or would have preferred to buy elsewhere in order to get what they did want—the franchise.

In the case of franchise tie-ins, franchisors may require their franchisees to buy certain items from them if the specifications for these products are a trade secret, or are too complex to entrust to others. For example, Carvel has successfully required its franchisees to purchase its soft ice cream mix, since the specifications for the mix are a closely guarded trade secret. Chicken Delight, in contrast, was not permitted to require its franchisees to buy paper cups and napkins from it, where a court found that it could have published specifications for these products and permitted its franchisees to purchase them from any source capable of meeting those specifications. If a trademark is identified with a specific *product*, as distinguished from an outlet, the franchisor may require franchisees to purchase that product only from him. Some examples are Baskin-Robbins ice cream and Shell gasoline. In addition, the franchisor generally may require franchisees to purchase certain items from unrelated companies if a sound business reason exists, so long as those companies do not pay anything to the franchisor. Since the franchisor stands to make no profit from such an arrangement, his motives presumably are to assure that his franchisees will carry only uniform, high-quality products. This is not considered a tie-in, because the supplier is not profiting from the sale of both products. Franchisees also may be permitted to propose additional sources for the franchisor's approval, in which case such approval should not be withheld unreasonably.

Tying Under the Guidelines.

The Justice Department's Vertical Restraints Guidelines include a section on tie-ins, establishing a separate test for screening tying cases. Under this test, the Department will presume that a tie-in is lawful if the seller has a market share of 30 percent or less in the market for the tying product.*

If the seller's market share is greater than 30 percent, the Department will apply a rule of reason analysis in determining whether to take action. The only exception is for a seller who has such "dominant" market power (which the Department defines as "akin to monopoly power") that the tie-in should be considered *per se* unlawful, in which case the Department can be expected to challenge it. Otherwise, the Guidelines take a decidedly tolerant approach to tying arrangements, observing that they "generally do not have a significant anticompetitive potential" and "often serve procompetitive or competitively neutral purposes." These purposes, according to the Department, can include protecting a supplier's reputation by tying his product to a maintenance contract or to sales of approved parts, "thus reduc[ing] the risk of inferior service by distributors." The Department also recognizes that tying may be particularly useful in introducing new products, because suppliers can keep the price of the new product low by tying in required sales of more established products, thereby sharing the risk that the new product will prove unpopular.

Remember: despite the apparent softening of the rules in this area, tie-ins still should be approached cautiously, particularly where one of the products involved has a significant market share. If a tie-in really is necessary or is especially desirable, it should only be crafted with the careful attention of counsel.

---

*The 30 percent figure corresponds to a market share examined by the Supreme Court in a recent tying decision, Jefferson Parish Hospital v. Hyde.

Full Line Forcing.

Sometimes a supplier may find it important for his dealers to carry his full line of products. Where a dealer is required to carry the full line, his freedom to choose his own inventory naturally is limited. Such "full line forcing" may not restrain the dealer as much as exclusive dealing, however, since the dealer remains free to carry competing brands, assuming that he has the facilities and enough business for this to be practical.

Full line forcing has not been treated as *per se* unlawful by the courts. Where the supplier can demonstrate a legitimate business need for his dealers to carry the full line, the restriction may well be upheld as reasonable, particularly where the quantities of each item which must be carried in inventory are also reasonable. For example, where a manufacturer relies upon wholesale distributors to supply retailers, it often is not unreasonable for the manufacturer to expect the wholesalers to have sufficient quantities of each of his products available in order to fill the retailers' orders promptly. Also, courts are likely to uphold requirements that dealers carry a representative line.

Restrictions on purchasing, as a group, are a mixed bag. Some, like exclusive dealing, are usually legal; some, like tying, are often not. Purchasing restrictions can be extremely important to a marketing program, because they permit the supplier to control what the dealers carry. Sometimes, however, they can prove to be volatile devices, particularly tying and full line forcing. They must be handled with care.

RESTRICTING SUPPLIERS' SALES

While most distribution restraints limit the freedom of dealers or other customers, some restraints limit the supplier. These limitations may be necessary in order to make the channel of distribution function efficiently. The most common restriction placed upon suppliers is the exclusive distributorship arrangement.

Exclusive Distributorships.

Exclusive distributorship agreements (sometimes known as "exclusive dealerships") prohibit suppliers from appointing more than one dealer within some defined territory, or from selling to more than one dealer in any given geographic area or market segment. An example appears in **Sample Provision 14.** An exclusive distributorship can promote competition by encouraging each dealer to make necessary investments, since it assures the dealer that no other dealers will be authorized in his area, and that the supplier will not begin to operate there either. An exclusive distributorship does not eliminate the possibility of invasions by dealers from other areas, unless there are also territorial restraints in place prohibiting such activities. Nevertheless, the exclusive distributorship assures the dealer that no other dealer of the same brand will actually set up shop nearby.

The Justice Department Guidelines take the position that exclusive distributorships are "clearly proper," and in fact almost every case has upheld them. Perhaps the best known was a case in which one of the only three Packard dealers in Baltimore demanded an exclusive distributorship for that city. Pack-

SAMPLE PROVISION 14
EXCLUSIVE DISTRIBUTORSHIP CLAUSE

Supplier will not sell to any other dealer located within Dealer's [territory] [area of primary responsibility] [, however, Supplier reserves the right to sell to the categories of customers listed in Exhibit A hereto,* regardless of where they are located].

---

*"Exhibit A" may list descriptions of customer categories, or may list specific customers, such as national account customers.

ard consented, terminating the other dealers, and these terminations were upheld by the court.

On a different level of distribution, Dakin, the stuffed animal importer, successfully enforced an exclusive disuribution agreement it had with a manufacturer in Korea. When one of Dakin's competitors attempted to purchase its own furry merchandise from the same manufacturer, Dakin prevented the sale, was sued, and won, with the court finding the arrangement reasonable.

Occasionally, an exclusive distribution arrangement may be created without any formal agreement at all. This happened to Whirlpool several years ago, and Whirlpool's story is a good example of how this can occur.

CASE HISTORY: Creating a Vacuum Exclusive.

Whirlpool Corporation, probably best known for manufacturing washing machines and other major appliances, also has been the producer of a line of vacuum cleaners. It began in 1957 by manufacturing vacuum cleaners exclusively for Sears, Roebuck and Company, which Sears sold under its "Kenmore" trademark. Six years later, after a few false starts, it also began producing vacuum cleaners bearing its own "Whirlpool" trademark. It sold these entirely to Oreck Corporation, which became the sole distributor for "Whirlpool" brand vacuum cleaners. The units which Whirlpool sold to Oreck were essentially the same as those which it sold to Sears.

Whirlpool expected Oreck to open up sales of its products to department stores and other retail outlets. At first, this is what Oreck did, but after a couple of years it began selling largely to janitorial supply houses instead. Two years later it also began selling directly to consumers by mail order, and within three years, these mail order sales constituted 90 percent of its business.

This turn of events met with displeasure at Whirlpool, and also at Sears. Sears personnel obtained copies of some of the direct mail advertising pieces which Oreck was regularly sending out to the public. These were forwarded to Whirlpool, and Sears indicated to Whirlpool that it considered Oreck's advertising to be improper. The advertising in question contained statements which allegedly were false and misleading, including a claim that the vacuum cleaners were being offered at half price.

A Whirlpool sales representative allegedly spoke with Oreck's president during the same period of time and expressed the view that Whirlpool's displeasure was attributable to the "other customer," which had its own well-known catalogue business and did not care for Oreck's mail order solicitation. This representative, according to Oreck's president, also expressed the opinion that Sears "got to the head of the company." When Oreck had tried to enter the Canadian market a year earlier, Whirlpool refused to make the necessary modifications to the machines so that they could be sold there. The same Whirlpool representative allegedly informed Oreck that this had occurred because Whirlpool could not "obtain a waiver to the current franchise," by which he allegedly meant that Whirlpool had been unable to secure approval from Sears.

The next time Oreck's distribution contract came up for renewal, Whirlpool refused to renew. Oreck suspected a conspiracy between Whirlpool and Sears to do it in and sued, raising some pointed questions:

1. Was Whirlpool making its own decision in declining to renew Oreck's contract, or was it just succumbing to pressure from Sears? Was Sears entitled to bring Oreck's questionable advertising claims to Whirlpool's attention? Was Sears asking for an exclusive distributorship?

2. Would it make any difference to know that Oreck's sales were on the increase at the end? That Sears was Whirlpool's largest customer and owned a sizeable block of Whirlpool's stock?

3. Was it legitimate for Whirlpool to be concerned about Oreck's abandonment of sales to retail outlets in favor of direct mail solicitation? Was it legitimate for Whirlpool to be concerned about loose claims made in Oreck's advertising? Would it make a difference that Whirlpool was receiving complaints about Oreck's advertising from other sources at the same time?

When one of only two dealers for a brand asks the supplier to discontinue dealing with his rival, this could be viewed as a request for an exclusive distributorship, regardless of whether the dealer making the request happens to use this particular terminology. Dealers ordinarily are entitled to request exclusive distributorships, even if their motivation is nothing more than to eliminate competition from other sellers of the same brand. The courts eventually found in favor of Whirlpool and Sears, although there was some strong dissent.

Output Contracts.

An output contract is an arrangement under which a producer agrees to sell his entire output of a product to a particular purchaser. Output arrangements often appear in conjunction with agreements by the purchaser to buy the seller's entire output. They also may contain provisions limiting the amount purchased and sold to no more than a stated maximum and no less than a stated minimum quantity. Normally, output contracts will be valid unless alternative supplies of the product are so scarce that the contract can unreasonably restrain trade or create a monopoly. An output provision can be agreed upon with language such as that in **Sample Provision 15.**

Output restrictions and exclusive distributorships are usually bargained-for agreements to which suppliers consent in order to gain or keep accounts. Any harm which may be done to competition affects other customers rather than other suppliers, and if litigation arises, it is usually the shut-out customers, including dealers, who sue.

SAMPLE PROVISION 15
OUTPUT PROVISION

Seller will sell and Buyer will purchase Seller's total output of gossamer for a period of _____ years, provided that in no one year will Seller have an output of less than _____ tons and that in no one year will Buyer be required to purchase more than _____ tons.

ALLOCATING IN A SHORTAGE

Recently, many businesses have become all too familiar with the problems of shortages. Raw materials become unavailable and production schedules cannot be met. The inevitable question is how to allocate the output which remains available and avoid being sued, particularly where the producer requires a portion of that output himself, for his own use.

The answer is to devise a fair and rational allocation plan, either well in advance or at least at the outset of the shortage situation, and stick to it. Where the Uniform Commercial Code applies (generally, to the sale of goods), Section 2-615(b) provides that, in a shortage, a seller:

> must allocate production and deliveries among his customers but may at his option include regular customers not then under contract as well as his own requirements for further manufacture. He may so allocate in any manner which is fair and reasonable.

In this connection, whatever allocation plan is adopted will gain in credibility if it is established early, memorialized, and adhered to. If there are written agreements with customers, the supplier can include a provision, such as **Sample Provision 16**, which explicitly reserves the right to allocate in any reasonable manner the supplier chooses.

In addition, it is important to inform customers of an allocation at the time it is put into effect, and assure each customer

SAMPLE PROVISION 16
ALLOCATION CLAUSE

Supplier reserves the right to allocate its inventory of Products in any manner as it may, in its sole discretion, determine at any time.

FORM 3
ALLOCATION LETTER

Dear Customer:

As you may already know, we have begun to suffer from the effects of the growing shortage of phlogiston which has been afflicting our industry in recent months. Because of this, we anticipate that we will not be able to meet our planned production schedules over the next six months and possibly longer, resulting in some delay in making deliveries.

I want to assure you, however, that every one of our customers will be treated fairly and equitably. We may be forced to deliver less than your full order at first, but if this becomes necessary, you can be assured that other customers will be receiving less than their full orders as well. Eventually, we hope to deliver all orders in full, and we will continue to accept orders for future deliveries, which we will schedule as more phlogiston becomes available.

I am sorry for any inconvenience this may be causing you, and I appreciate your understanding in getting through these difficult times.

Sincerely,

_____

that he is being treated fairly. This can be done by letter, such as the announcement in **Form 3.**

Inevitably, some customers will request preferential treatment, and the supplier must be careful not to upset the fairness of the allocation. The pressures can be enormous, of course, and there is no way to make everyone happy in these situations. Relations between suppliers and dealers can be difficult enough in the best of times, and shortage situations put these relationships to the ultimate test.

A right-to-allocate clause has the value of creating greater certainty for both the supplier and the dealer regarding the nature of their relationship and their respective obligations. This is something that all the provisions described in this chapter should accomplish. No distribution agreement is perfect. No distribution agreement can anticipate every eventuality which will arise over the course of a relationship. But by specifying what each party may or may not do, a well-drafted agreement can prevent a good deal of squabbling later, and keep the focus of the relationship where it belongs—on building sales.

Putting together a distribution contract can be a little like choosing dishes from a menu. You have to know what's available before you can order. If the marketing executive knows the full spectrum of provisions he can choose from, and his lawyer knows what the executive is trying to achieve, together they will be better equipped to assemble a contract that meets the requirements of the marketing program without creating unnecessary legal risks. Drafting contracts is not fun, and no contract ever won a Pulitzer Prize. But bad contracts lose lawsuits, and the extra effort devoted to getting your distribution agreements right the first time will never be regretted.

Four

TERMINATING
DEALERS

We turn now to the world of high drama and high stakes litigation—terminating existing dealers. In almost every distribution network there will be some dealer somewhere who is not performing up to par in certain respects, or who otherwise no longer fits into the supplier's marketing scheme. The supplier may try warnings; he may try giving additional support; he may even try both. But sometimes the results remain discouraging and the decision eventually is made to sever the relationship.

Suppliers must proceed with caution—terminations can be fraught with peril. In fact, there is probably no other situation which presents the marketing executive with so many opportunities to step on legal landmines. Yet terminations occur every day, and they can be completed without violating any laws if a number of guidelines are followed attentively. A good illustration, and a good place to begin this chapter, is the experience of Riddell.

CASE HISTORY: Booting Out a Football Dealer.

One of the best known names on the gridiron in recent seasons has been Riddell, a manufacturer of football helmets, shoes and other athletic equipment. Riddell distributed its products through a network of independent retail dealers, each of whom was required under written agreements to provide certain pre-sale and post-sale services. Riddell was particularly sensitive about service because if its equipment was not fitted properly and repaired correctly, the company could be exposed to catastrophic personal injury lawsuits. Football helmet suppliers have been faced with an enormous amount of such litigation over the past few years.

Riddell also went a step further and placed a restriction on each dealer forbidding him from selling Riddell products to anyone except consumers and other authorized dealers. "Bootlegging" to unauthorized outlets was prohibited. Riddell's strategy, in effect, was to provide each of its dealers with a zone of protection so that Riddell could demand and receive dedicated service from each of them in return.

At one point, representatives of Riddell met with a number of the dealers as a group and explained the bootlegging policy to them. There was a lengthy discussion, in the course of which the dealers were asked to report any instances of suspected bootlegging to Riddell. They were given assurances that their reports would be investigated, and that steps would be taken to halt any bootlegging which was uncovered.

Before long, one of these dealers discovered that a nearby department store, which was not authorized by Riddell, was selling Riddell football shoes to a local college. The dealer reported this incident to Riddell, which commenced an investigation. It turned out that a neighboring Riddell dealer, The Sports Center, had sold the shoes to the department store for resale to the college. Riddell's management discussed the situation internally and decided to terminate The Sports Center as an authorized dealer. Riddell's Vice President of Sales sent The Sports Center the following letter:

> It has come to our attention that you have violated one of the basic requirements of being a Riddell dealer by providing products to unauthorized accounts.
>
> We have no other alternative, therefore, but to exercise our option under Paragraph 2 in your dealer agreement cancelling you as an authorized Riddell dealer effective immediately.
>
> We are sorry that your relationship with Riddell didn't mean enough to you to protect the franchise and operate

within the rules. We appreciate your business in 1976 and wish you the best of luck in the future.

The Sports Center did not take this news well and sued, raising these questions:

1. May a supplier deputize his dealers to report infractions of his sales restrictions by other dealers? May the supplier discuss his policy on this subject with the dealers as a group?

2. May a supplier terminate a dealer who has violated the supplier's marketing policies after receiving complaints about these violations from another dealer?

3. Should a dealer who detects violations by other dealers report them to the supplier? Should the dealer discuss these violations with other dealers first? Should he try to work things out with the offending dealer directly?

Dealers can be an important source of information for the supplier, and as long as the supplier makes his own decision whether or not to terminate, the receipt of information from the dealers should not give rise to a conspiracy. The court found that Riddell's customer restrictions were reasonable, and that its termination of The Sports Center was reasonable too. If dealers themselves become the decision-makers, however, or try to take matters into their own hands, the result may be different. You have to follow the rules to avoid the penalties, and learning those rules is what the rest of this chapter is all about.

REASONS FOR TERMINATION

We start with the premise that there are numerous legitimate reasons for terminating dealers. Perhaps the most common is poor sales performance. An equally basic reason is failure to pay for merchandise on time. Dealers commonly order their inventory on credit, and the law generally recognizes the right of a supplier to terminate dealers who pay late.

Other reasons are equally legitimate. Suppliers may stop selling to dealers who fail to maintain their premises in a presentable manner or who fail to treat customers properly. In one instance, an oil company successfully litigated a case in which it was sued by a service station operator it had dropped after receiving reports that the station's employees were in the habit of making coarse and abusive remarks to customers. Dealers also may be terminated for dishonest conduct, including misuse of the suppliers' trademarks or trade secrets.

In many cases, as we have seen, suppliers are entitled to impose selling and purchasing restraints on their dealers, such as restrictions on where the dealers may sell, the customers to whom they may sell and the types of competing merchandise they may carry. So long as these restrictions are permissible, dealers may be terminated if they violate them. For example, if a dealer is limited to selling a supplier's products only to authorized customers, but begins selling them to other customers as well, the supplier normally may terminate the dealer. This is what happened in the case of Riddell, and the court held that it was reasonable. Likewise, in the landmark *Sylvania* case, decided in 1977, Sylvania stopped selling its television sets to a dealer who refused to abide by a requirement that he sell them only from an authorized location. The dealer sued and Sylvania eventually won a victory before the United States Supreme Court which established an important precedent. If the restraint on the dealer is permissible in the first place, termination for violating the restraint will generally be permissible as well.

Wholly apart from any unsatisfactory conduct on the part of the dealers, suppliers may terminate dealers simply because the supplier has decided he no longer wants to sell through independent dealers at all, or because he wants to abandon a certain geographic area entirely. In all of these cases, however, the right to terminate may be limited by contractual rights or by special franchise legislation where it applies.

Creating Exclusive Distributorships.

A supplier occasionally will terminate a dealer in order to give another dealer what is called an "exclusive distributorship" or "exclusive dealership." This is a limitation on the supplier himself, rather than the dealers, under which the supplier promises a particular dealer that he will not appoint any other dealers to serve a defined geographic territory or a defined category of customers. Exclusive distributorships are almost always considered lawful.

Also, it normally is permissible for the dealer himself to ask for an exclusive distributorship, even if this would require the supplier to terminate other dealers already serving the desired market. This is what happened in the Packard automobile case described in the last chapter, and in the case of Whirlpool and Sears. If an exclusive distributorship is lawful, accompanying terminations will be considered lawful as well, with two cautions. First, any special franchise legislation, or explicit contractual rights forbidding termination, must be taken into account. Second, the dealer making the request must be asking for genuine exclusivity. If he is merely asking the supplier to eliminate some unwanted competition from certain other dealers, without making him the *only* dealer for the brand in the territory, terminations pursuant to his request are likely to be considered illegal. Where the dealer really is asking for an exclusive, however, the terminations generally will be permissible.

Illegal Terminations.

So what's the problem? Why do so many terminated dealers still sue their suppliers? One answer is that they hope to get injunctions ordering their reinstatement, together with treble damages and payment of their attorney's fees. If a dealer's suit is successful, the court can order the dealer reinstated, and can award him treble the amount of his lost profits, or treble the value of his business if he has gone out of business, together with attorney's fees and other litigation costs. Another reason there are so many suits is that terminations can and do run afoul of the law in a variety of ways, giving some terminated dealers legitimate grounds to complain and recover. This leads inevitably to the next question: When is it *not* legal to terminate a dealer?

There are several answers, but essentially most come down to price fixing. The most common allegation in lawsuits brought by terminated dealers against former suppliers is that regardless of appearances, the dealer really was terminated for cutting prices. As noted earlier, resale price maintenance (i.e., control of prices at subsequent levels of distribution) is illegal. It is *per se* illegal, meaning that if the dealer can prove that resale prices were being fixed pursuant to agreement, and that the termination was a means of enforcing that agreement, virtually no defenses will be recognized.

If a dealer can prove that he really was terminated for failure to adhere to resale prices dictated by his supplier, the termination almost certainly will be found illegal, except in the rare case where the narrow channel of lawful conduct charted by the Supreme Court in the *Colgate* case can be navigated. But that can be like passing between Scylla and Charybdis. If the dealer can show that he previously had *agreed* with the supplier to fix prices—that there had been a "meeting of the minds"—the dealer will be able to argue that he was terminated for breaking that illegal agreement, and that the protection of *Colgate* should evaporate. Likewise, if the dealer can show that other dealers had agreed to maintain prices, and that his termination was designed to shield those other dealers from discounting pursuant to their agreements with the supplier, the protection of *Colgate* also will disappear.

Price fixing need not always be involved, however, in order for a termination to be illegal. If other restrictions, such as restrictions on where a dealer may sell, are themselves so unreasonable that they violate the law under the "rule of reason" described earlier, terminations of dealers for disregarding these restrictions also can be held illegal. Under the rule of reason, courts will examine all of the procompetitive and anticompetitive effects of a restraint, and attempt to balance them against one another in order to determine whether the restraint is reasonable.

Again, the dealer in a case like this actually must be able to prove that he agreed to the restriction previously, and then was terminated for violating that agreement. Or, he must be able to prove a conspiracy involving other dealers. Several cases also have suggested that if a dealer is coerced to adhere to an illegal restriction, such as resale price maintenance, but refuses and is then terminated, he can sue on this basis alone, even though he never actually agreed to participate. Whether this remains true today is open to question, but a prudent supplier will avoid leaving himself open to this argument in the first place.

Conspiracies to Terminate.

Wholly apart from the problem of enforcing illegal sales restrictions, terminations can also be illegal when they are made in response to pressure from other dealers. It is an almost universal practice for dealers to complain to their suppliers about the activities of other dealers of the same brand, particularly when it comes to price cutting. In fact, the United States Supreme Court recognized in the recent case of *Monsanto* v. *Spray Rite* that it is "natural" and "unavoidable" for dealers to complain about one another to their common supplier. If these complaints are relied on by the supplier for purposes of enforcing his own legitimate marketing objectives, as in the case of Riddell, this will present no problem. If the supplier succumbs to these complaints to terminate a dealer he otherwise would have chosen to retain, however, there is a good chance that his actions will be held unlawful. Courts will view this as a conspiracy between the supplier and the complaining dealer or dealers to reduce competition at the dealer level—unless, as noted earlier, a single complaining dealer is legitimately asking for an exclusive distributorship in a particular territory.

The most difficult situation arises where the supplier, in his own judgment, has decided to terminate a dealer who also is the subject of complaints. This can be tricky. For example, if several dealers complain to the supplier that another dealer, "Poor Richard's Bargain Basement," has been violating local health and safety codes and tarnishing the image of the brand in the process, the supplier may want to terminate Poor Richard on the ground that, in the supplier's own judgment, the supplier does not want to deal with anyone who displays his products in a filthy or unsafe environment. This should be perfectly lawful because the complaining dealers are merely reporting information, rather than convincing the supplier to take action against his better judgment. The Supreme Court itself pointed out in *Monsanto* that dealers commonly serve as "an important source of information" for their supplier.

But Poor Richard may also be a discounter. This, in fact, may upset the other dealers even more. The other dealers may complain to the supplier that Poor Richard has been cutting prices. The supplier may investigate and discover that Poor Richard can afford to cut prices precisely because he has been neglecting the local health and safety codes. The supplier may not care particularly about the prices Poor Richard charges, but may proceed to terminate Poor Richard on the basis of the code violations. If the supplier is exercising his own judgment, the termination should be lawful—but you can lay odds that it will look like a price fixing conspiracy to Poor Richard. Legality will depend on whether the decision-makers within the supplier's organization really were exercising their own judgment, or were simply succumbing to dealer complaints.

The Supreme Court addressed this question in the *Monsanto* case and concluded that a supplier should not be barred from terminating a dealer for legitimate reasons simply because other dealers have been complaining about that dealer's pricing. The Court observed:

> To bar a manufacturer from acting solely because the information upon which it acts originated as a price complaint would create an irrational dislocation in the market.

The Court went on to explain that to find illegality,

> something more than evidence of complaints is needed. There must be evidence that tends to exclude the possibility that the manufacturer and nonterminated distributors were acting independently.

This kind of evidence may not be easy for a terminated dealer to find. But it is not impossible—in the *Monsanto* case itself, the Court found "smoking gun" evidence of a price fixing agreement between the supplier and some of the remaining dealers, and ruled in favor of the dealer who had been terminated. The damning evidence showed that on at least two occasions, Monsanto had threatened not to deliver adequate supplies to dealers if they would not stop cutting prices. And when one of these dealers refused to raise his prices, Monsanto went directly to that dealer's parent company, which instructed the dealer to comply. The dealer afterward assured Monsanto that he would hold the line, sealing the unlawful agreement.

How to Proceed.

So how should a supplier contemplating a termination proceed? First, it may be appropriate to respond to dealer complaints, if there are any. The supplier can contact the complaining dealer or dealers and make clear that his decision will be entirely unilateral. An example of such a communication is provided in **Form 4.**

Next, the supplier must address the dealer who is going to be terminated. An advisable preliminary step here is to check the accounts receivable file and attempt to bring the dealer's account current before breaking the bad news. Otherwise, there may be a long wait until any more is collected. Suppliers should avoid terminating a dealer who owes substantial amounts of money unless there is no prospect that the account will become current anytime soon.

Then, the supplier normally should write to the dealer and notify him of the termination. The supplier also may decide to visit in person, in hopes of defusing any explosive reactions. The wording of the termination letter is important, and will depend upon whether there have been prior warnings and whether the supplier chooses to detail his reasons for reaching his decision. Exactly how much detail to include in a letter of this kind will be determined by the circumstances of each situ-

FORM 4
RESPONSE TO COMPLAINING DEALER

CERTIFIED MAIL
RETURN RECEIPT REQUESTED

Existing Dealer
101 Main Street
Anywhere, U.S.A. 12345

Dear Dealer:

Our District Manager, Mr. Efficient, has reported to me that you recently informed him that Poor Richard's Bargain Basement appears to be violating our operating standards for dealers. You also apparently requested that Poor Richard be terminated as a dealer.

As you know, our decisions in terminating dealers are ours alone. While you have expressed your concern, we will be guided by our own business judgment in making this determination. Whether or not we act, the decision will be unilateral.

Very truly yours,

_____

ation. There is no one "right" approach for all eventualities, and consultation with a lawyer at this point is normally prudent. The amount of detail to include in the letter also may be governed by any special termination laws which apply in particular circumstances. Additionally, the letter may offer various options for disposing of inventory. In any event, the letter should be unequivocal, such as that illustrated by **Form 5.** A copy of the letter should be retained in case there is litigation.

SPECIAL TERMINATION LAWS

Over the years, there has been a perception among some legislators at both the state and federal levels that once a dealer has invested his money and his energy in the marketing of a particular brand, he should be protected against termination by the supplier of that brand except for good cause. This perception has prompted the enactment of various pieces of legislation restricting the supplier's prerogative to terminate dealers. Special termination laws also may dictate the type of notice which suppliers are required to furnish prior to termination.

At the federal level, the Automobile Dealer Franchise Act (commonly called the "Dealer Day in Court Act") requires auto manufacturers to act in good faith whenever terminating or refusing to renew a dealer franchise. The federal Petroleum Marketing Practices Act prohibits termination or nonrenewal of franchises granted to petroleum dealers except under specified circumstances. The provisions of both acts are fairly specific, and unless a number of prerequisites are met in each instance, the acts will not apply.

At the state level, a diverse variety of legislation directed at terminations is now on the books. Some states have laws covering only specific industries, such as beer, wine, farm equipment and, again, automobiles and petroleum products. Other states have broader statutes which apply to any dealer relationship which the state law defines as a "franchise." Still other states have no termination laws at all.

While the application and the requirements of these enactments vary enormously, virtually all forbid franchisors from terminating or failing to renew a franchise without some type of good cause. Most also require that franchisees be provided some form of written notice prior to termination, specifying the franchisor's reasons for taking action. Some of the laws assure

FORM 5
TERMINATION LETTER

CERTIFIED MAIL
RETURN RECEIPT REQUESTED

Substandard Shop
100 Backstreet
Nowhere, U.S.A. 10987

Dear Dealer:

This is to advise you that we will no longer accept orders from you and that your dealership is hereby terminated. We regret that your persistent failure to meet our standards has resulted in this action.

While you may continue to sell the merchandise you have on hand, I would be willing to discuss the possible alternative of our repurchasing your inventory at a mutually agreeable price. In any event, you may not continue to use our trademarks except for purposes of disposing of existing inventory.

We have afforded you a fair opportunity to meet our standards. Unfortunately, you have failed to meet them. As a consequence, we are exercising our right to continue dealing only with those dealers which, in our judgment, are willing and able to perform up to those standards.

Very truly yours,

_____

the franchisees a period of time in which to cure their defaults, with the exception of such incurable indiscretions as fraud, criminal activity or bankruptcy. Normally, "good cause" for termination will be defined broadly enough to include such routine grounds as failure by the franchisee adequately to serve an assigned territory, engaging in deceptive sales practices or other unsatisfactory performance. But each law is different, and the statutes must be consulted on a case-by-case basis. A few examples of the statutes' provisions are listed on pages 86 and 87.

Often, the most controversial issue involving these laws is the definition of the term "franchise" itself. The broader the definition, the broader the applicability of the law will be. Some courts have applied these laws even to sales representatives who make little or no investment of their own, while other courts have limited the reach of these laws to full-service dealers who actually do business under the franchisor's trademark.

The difficulty this presents for marketing executives who operate on a national or even regional level is a pronounced lack of uniformity and predictability. If a supplier's relationships with his dealers can be considered "franchises" in any of the states in which he does business, the special requirements of notice, opportunity to cure and good cause all may apply to decisions to terminate in those states. Failure to comply with the letter of law may leave the supplier surprised to discover that the dealer he thought he had terminated last month is still aboard, and mad as hell. These franchising laws can be complicated and bothersome for suppliers, but they simply cannot be overlooked if terminations are to be successful.

Selecting and terminating dealers are really two sides of the same coin. Executives who understand what the law demands will find that they can be guided by the same legal principles in both types of situations, and be on the right track every time.

EXCERPTS FROM
SELECTED TERMINATION LAWS

Automobile Dealer Franchise Act (1956)

Requires automobile manufacturers to act in "good faith" in performing any of the terms of their franchise agreements, or in terminating or refusing to renew such agreements. Good faith is defined as acting in a "fair and equitable manner," without using "coercion, intimidation, or threats of coercion or intimidation"; but this does not preclude the use of "recommendations, endorsement, exposition, persuasion, urging or argument."

Petroleum Marketing Practices Act (1978)

Prohibits suppliers of motor fuel from terminating or refusing to renew a franchise relationship except under specified circumstances, including failure of the franchisee to comply with reasonable and material provisions of the franchise agreement or to exercise good faith in carrying out such provisions, certain types of changed circumstances in the relationship, repeated consumer complaints, and the franchisee's failure to maintain clean and safe premises.

California Franchise Relations Act, Section 20020 (1980)

"Except as otherwise provided by this chapter, no franchisor may terminate a franchise prior to the expiration of its term, except for good cause. Good cause shall include, but not be limited to, the failure of the franchisee to comply with any lawful requirement of the franchise agreement after being given notice thereof and a reasonable opportunity, which in no event need be more than 30 days, to cure the failure."

Subsequent sections of the Act set out a series of "reasonable grounds for termination," on which a supplier may terminate a franchisee immediately. There is also a California law, Section 20025 of the same Act, placing certain limitations on a franchisor's discretion to refuse to renew a franchise.

Wisconsin Fair Dealership Law, Sections 135.03-135.045
Cancellation and Alteration of Dealerships
"Sec. 135.03. No grantor, directly or through any officer, agent or employee, may terminate, cancel, fail to renew or substantially change the competitive circumstances of a dealership agreement without good cause. The burden of proving good cause is on the grantor."

Notice of Termination or Change in Dealership
"Sec. 135.04. Except as provided in this section, a grantor shall provide a dealer at least 90 days' prior written notice of termination, cancellation, nonrenewal or substantial change in competitive circumstances. The notice shall state all the reasons for termination, cancellation, nonrenewal or substantial change in competitive circumstances and shall provide that the dealer has 60 days in which to rectify any claimed deficiency. If the deficiency is rectified within 60 days the notice shall be void. The notice provisions of this section shall not apply if the reason for termination, cancellation or nonrenewal is insolvency, the occurrence of an assignment for the benefit of creditors or bankruptcy. If the reason for termination, cancellation, nonrenewal or substantial change in competitive circumstances is nonpayment of sums due under the dealership, the dealer shall be entitled to written notice of such default, and shall have 10 days in which to remedy such default from the date of delivery or posting of such notice."

Repurchase of Inventories
"Sec. 135.045. If a dealership is terminated by the grantor, the grantor, at the option of the dealer, shall repurchase all inventories sold by the grantor to the dealer for resale under the dealership agreement at the fair wholesale market value. This section applies only to merchandise with a name, trademark, label or other mark on it which identifies the grantor."

Five

DETERMINING PRICES

Price fixing is the cardinal sin of antitrust. It is treated as a *per se* offense, meaning that virtually no justification will be recognized. It may be prosecuted as a felony, and courts have not hesitated to assess steep fines and prison sentences on transgressors.

Marketing executives frequently carry price setting authority. From the vice president who approves each new price list to the sales representative exercising discretion to offer discounts to particular customers, marketing personnel are regularly called upon to make pricing decisions.

This chapter will describe how to make those decisions without going to jail. We will look first at how the supplier may set his own prices and then focus on what influence the supplier is entitled to exert over the prices charged by his dealers.

ARRIVING AT THE SELLING PRICE

Naturally, the primary decision which sellers at all levels of distribution must make is what to charge for their products. Pricing decisions are highly sensitive, often seeming to combine statistics with metaphysics. Economists are fond of charting "optimal" price levels for maximizing profits based on the laws of supply and demand. For the marketing director faced with choosing a price for a new product or adjusting the price for an existing product, however, economic theory is of limited value since the data needed to calculate the "optimal" price is never available. Instead, the marketing director must rely on experience, instinct and whatever data is, in fact, on hand to come up with a price. There usually is a lot riding on the decision, of course. Positioning a product in terms of price is critical, and most pricing decisions, once made, are difficult and expensive to revise.

The law places important limits on pricing determinations. First and foremost, a seller may not arrive at prices by colluding with his competitors either directly or indirectly. Also, a supplier who sells to dealers may not freely discriminate in the prices he charges to dealers who compete with one another, but must adhere to certain limits which the law places on price discrimination. The rules may seem complex at times, but the consequences for ignoring them can be catastrophic.

Considering Competitors' Prices.

Prices cannot be set in a vacuum. Prices also cannot be set by phoning your competitors and agreeing on what everyone should charge. Between these two extremes lies a broad range of options for lawfully arriving at a competitive price.

Phoning your competitor to discuss prices should never take place at any level, from sales representative to president. Not only are you likely to get caught eventually, your competitor himself may turn you in. The president of American Airlines reportedly called the president of Braniff recently and said, "Raise your goddamn fares 20 percent. I'll raise mine the next morning." The Braniff president recorded the conversation and blew the whistle. (The Government sued American and its president. The complaint was upheld by an appellate court, and American consented to a decree barring such conduct in the future.)

Other price fixing invitations have met with more receptive responses, of course. Such conspiracies often are accompanied by elaborate mechanisms for avoiding detection. For example, in the highly publicized electrical equipment conspiracy cases some years ago, the evidence showed that the manufacturers of electric power generators rigged their bids for upcoming contracts under a formula which predetermined the winner of each contract based on the phases of the moon. Nevertheless, many conspiracies are detected, and a substantial number of regular, everyday marketing executives have paid large fines and gone to jail. It is a mistake to think that because no drugs or violence are involved, the Justice Department does not view price fixing as a serious crime. While there have been differences in other aspects of antitrust enforcement philosophy from one administration to the next over the years, the war on price fixing among competitors has been constant.

Naturally, competitors' prices cannot be ignored. While the law will not permit price fixing, there is no legal impediment to the necessary process of monitoring competitors' prices and pricing your own products at an appropriate level in relation to those prices, taking into account differences in quality, performance, capabilities, brand, size, and so on. This is the very essence of competition.

Price Signalling.

Complications may develop, however, from a phenomenon sometimes termed "price signalling." Competitors in certain industries occasionally have been criticized for "signalling" one another about price changes in advance of implementation, permitting the competitors to "follow the leader" and adjust their own prices, often effective on the same date. This can be particularly significant in the case of price increases, since the leader can test the waters by announcing an upcoming price increase and waiting to see whether the major competitors in the industry will follow, or will be underpricing him after the increase goes into effect. If no one else in the industry follows the lead, the price increase can still be rescinded before it is scheduled to take effect, without any significant loss of sales.

Is price signalling illegal? Usually not, but in special circumstances it may be. As the law has developed, the mere act of announcing price changes in advance is not unlawful, even in a market with few sellers. There are legitimate reasons for making such announcements, particularly to allow customers to stock up at the old price, thereby cushioning the impact of price increases and building volume at the same time. Once there is proof of an ongoing understanding among the sellers regarding how they will react to such announcements, however, illegality may attach.

Price Reporting.

Another sensitive area is price reporting. In some industries everyone knows everyone else's prices, but in other industries there is so much price variation that no seller can be sure of what prices other sellers are charging from one week to the next. While uncertainty of this kind can have the effect of stimulating price competition, the kind of competition generated is fueled largely by rumors and guesswork. In the economists' model of perfect competition, by contrast, there is perfect information, with every seller informed of all current market prices. This information, as the theory goes, permits each seller to set a competitive price. In the real world too, knowledge of competitors' prices can result in more competitive pricing by all sellers as long as there is no collusion, and certain forms of price reporting are therefore permissible.

This is treacherous territory, however, and one false step can bring down an avalanche of lawsuits. Often, trade associations are involved, and while these associations provide many important, legitimate services, they also can become "walking conspiracies" when they begin serving as clearinghouses for price information. Price reporting arrangements must follow certain rules scrupulously, and a lawyer should be overseeing every decision like a nervous babysitter.

First, only the prices charged in past transactions should be reported. If it's not yet history, don't report it. Second, there should be no forecasts, projections or speculation of any kind—nothing that can serve as a suggestion of what prices anyone should charge in the future. Third, individual sellers should not be identified, if at all possible. This can be accomplished by having each seller report to an independent outsider, such as an accounting firm, which will aggregate the figures or otherwise put them into a format in which individual sellers cannot be identified. Fourth, every seller in the industry should be included, if they want to be. Fifth, and most important, there cannot be any agreement among sellers as to prices to be charged in the future, how prices will be quoted in the future, or any other terms of sale. Price reporting should remain passive and retrospective.

Nobody said that deciding on prices is easy. The bottom line is never to *agree* with any competitor in any manner about prices to be charged or any other term of sale affecting the value of the sales transaction. Price determinations should be made in solitude, not at industry meetings in airport hotels.

Selling Below Cost.

With so much popular attention continually being paid to price gouging and conspiracies to raise prices, it may seem bizarre that a seller also can get hammered for charging too little—but in certain circumstances he can. The terms "predatory pricing" and "below cost pricing" refer to the practice of selling a product for less than the cost of manufacturing it or otherwise obtaining it. Where the purpose behind such seemingly self-destructive behavior is to drive other sellers out of the market, or prevent new sellers from entering, and where the seller already has a major share of the market, this may be considered an attempt to monopolize, illegal under section 2 of the Sherman Act.

Courts have not had an easy time figuring out what "cost" a price must fall below in order to qualify as predatory. Economists suggest "marginal cost," the cost of producing one additional unit at a given level of output. But "marginal cost" is an economist's concept, which almost never can actually be calculated. Most courts look instead to short-term average variable cost, a figure which can be calculated using principles of cost accounting. If a seller is charging a price which at least covers his variable costs (such as raw materials, labor, etc.), and maybe some of his fixed costs (such as rent, heat and other overhead), courts usually will not consider his prices predatory. On the other hand, if a seller is charging a price so low that he is not even covering all of his variable costs, most courts will presume that such activity is predatory, absent evidence of a legitimate business purpose such as entering a market, meeting competition or liquidating a discontinued model.

Selling below variable cost is presumed to be undertaken with an anticompetitive motive because otherwise it would be irrational—the seller would be better off producing nothing at all than losing more and more as he increases production. In contrast, selling below total cost but above variable cost makes sense, at least in the short run, because although the seller may not be earning a profit, he is at least covering his variable costs, and the more he sells, the more of his fixed costs he can cover as well.

In order to violate section 2 of the Sherman Act, a seller must not only sell below cost, but have either monopoly power or at least a dangerous probability of achieving a monopoly. Usually, a seller who can sustain a period of predatory pricing does command considerable market power or there would be no point to engaging in the practice to begin with. Moreover, in some twenty-five states, selling below cost is illegal regardless of the likelihood of the seller achieving a monopoly. Several other states have similar laws applying only to certain industries. There is also a seldom heard of provision in the Robinson-Patman Act making it a crime to sell at "unreasonably low prices" for the purpose of destroying competition or eliminating a competitor, but there is no private right of action under this law and the Government has almost never tried to enforce it.

Often, sellers have no idea whether they are selling a product below cost at any particular point in time until they are sued, and years later they prepare a cost analysis. If a product is generating profits there normally will never be a problem of predatory pricing, but when prices are cut and profits begin to disappear, a review of the situation may be in order.

Establishing More Than One Selling Price.

One of the more nagging problems for some suppliers in determining prices is the pressure to offer favorable prices to preferred customers. While this is a common practice in some parts of the world, it is limited in the United States by the Robinson-Patman Act. This Act is sufficiently confusing that anyone who professes to know it all is probably lying, and any executive who tries to tackle it on his own is probably crazy.

The Robinson-Patman Act was passed in 1936, largely to protect small grocers and other small retailers from the enormous buying power of the major chains, most notably A&P, which attracted a great deal of attention at that time. The Act prohibits the supplier of a product from discriminating in price or in the provision of services among customers who resell the product in competition with one another. Certain defenses are available, however, including meeting competition.

Under the provisions of this Act, a supplier engaged in interstate commerce may not substantially injure competition by charging one price to some dealers, while charging a lower price for the goods of like grade and quality to other dealers competing for the same customers. All of the following elements must be present for the Act to apply: interstate commerce; actual, completed sales at different prices; discrimination between dealers who compete with one another; and tangible goods or "commodities," which must be of like grade and quality. And, there must be a substantial adverse injury to competition. When the Act does apply, it can reach buyers as well as sellers. A dealer is not permitted knowingly to induce his suppliers to sell at discriminatory prices.

All this does not mean that sellers are rigidly bound to charging only one price. There are a number of important exceptions to the Act which may apply, providing the seller considerable flexibility. The most important of these is known as the "meeting competition defense."

Meeting Competition.

Let's say you are the Vice President for Sales, and one of your top sales representatives calls to report that Colossus Industries, your largest dealer, has just been quoted a lower price by Dirt Cheap Imports, a major importer. Colossus is threatening to switch suppliers unless you can come across with a lower price. You know that you can drop your price significantly and still clear a profit—and you need the volume to keep the factory humming.

But some lawyer once told you about the Robinson-Patman Act. Can you charge Colossus a lower price than anyone else without breaking the law? The answer is "yes," but you have to do it right. The law permits a seller to meet the prices of his competitors, but the seller first must make an effort to verify the fact that the competing offer has been made, and its amount. This is important, because while it is lawful to meet a competitive offer, it is not permissible knowingly to *beat* that offer with an even lower price.

Verification.

How do you verify another seller's offer? One way is to call the seller and try asking, but this would be a mistake because it can give rise to charges of collusion. The proper practice is to ask the dealer. If a dealer wants you to meet another seller's lower price, he should be willing to tell you who that seller is and what price is being offered. You can also send the dealer a letter, confirming his description of the offer. A letter of this kind can be phrased with language such as that shown in **Form 6.**

Despite a request for such verification, dealers sometimes remain coy and refuse to disclose the exact amount of the offer

FORM 6
MEETING COMPETITION LETTER

CERTIFIED MAIL
RETURN RECEIPT REQUESTED

Mr. Willy Pickett
Colossus Industries, Inc.
10 Behemoth Boulevard
Elsewhere, U.S.A. 99999

Dear Willy:

On April 1 you informed me that Dirt Cheap Imports offered your company a price of twelve dollars ($12.00) per unit for their "Blowhard" brand inflatable attorneys, f.o.b. your warehouse, for minimum orders of one hundred (100) units, with no commitment on your part to purchase more than an initial order. (Please confirm this by signing below and returning this letter to me.) As I indicated to you previously, we would be willing to meet Dirt Cheap's offer with our "Vested Avenger" line, which is a comparable product.

I think you will agree that our product is the better choice. I look forward to hearing from you.

Very truly yours,

_____

Confirmed: _____

they have received. The dealer may simply announce that he has received a better offer and leave it up to the supplier to make a counteroffer, to which the dealer may respond, "You're not even in the ball park," and let the supplier try again. The dealer, of course, wants the supplier to drop the price as low as he is willing to go.

This puts the supplier in a difficult position. He may be able to improve his offer and still realize a profit, but he will be in the dark as to whether he is meeting the competitive offer or actually going even lower. He wants to keep the customer but does not want to violate the law.

Fortunately, the Supreme Court has addressed this thorny problem in a case* in which the FTC accused a buyer of inducing price discrimination. The buyer, ironically, was A&P again. The Court held that so long as the supplier makes a good faith effort to inquire about a competitive offer and meet it, the supplier does not violate the law even if he estimates incorrectly and actually beats the competitive offer. The seller, of course, may not contact his competitor to inquire about the terms of the competing offer, nor does he have to insist that the dealer disclose the precise terms. The dealer, for his part, may not mislead the seller too far, or he will be considered a "lying" buyer and open himself up to charges of inducing discriminatory pricing. This threat to the buyer provides some assurance that the seller will not be led very far astray, and that his counteroffer will merely be "meeting" competition.

All of these cautions apply equally to discrimination in services or facilities. Normally, these must be made available to all competing customers, large or small, on a "proportionally equal" basis, so that all can take advantage of them. Sometimes, however, certain favored customers may be provided with advertising allowances, display materials, live demonstrators or other services or facilities which other competing customers do not receive. If these are provided to meet a competing offer, they will be permissible. But again, the supplier must first make a good faith effort to verify the other offer.

---

*Great Atlantic & Pacific Tea Co. v. FTC.

In addition, note that a supplier can meet competition on an areawide basis, so that if a competitor is offering lower prices or greater services to all customers in an entire geographic region, the first supplier may offer the same terms to buyers in that region too, without having to make the same offer in any other region. Also, a supplier sometimes may simply adopt a pricing system used by a competitor lock, stock and barrel, as a means of meeting competition, and this too is normally permitted. Again, the supplier must be able to document that a competing offer was being met.

Documentation is not a detail. All too frequently, the circumstances surrounding the competing offer and the steps taken to meet it are not well documented and no adequate record is made or kept. Years later, when somebody sues and the supplier endeavors to prove that he acted properly, memories have faded and no one is sure of who supposedly made the other offer, what its terms reportedly were, or what steps were taken to verify it. One way to combat this problem is routinely to use a form collecting and preserving the pertinent information. This assures that the necessary steps are taken before the supplier makes a counter-offer, and creates a record which should be retained. Various formats are possible, including the example which appears as **Form 7.** Not all of the information on that form is required, but the more information you have, the easier it will be to prove that you were really meeting competition. The test is that a reasonably prudent executive would believe that the competing offer was being met and not beaten.

Other Defenses.

There are other defenses, beside "meeting competition," which also may be raised in Robinson-Patman Act cases, but these are often even more difficult to establish. One is the so-called "cost justification" defense. A particular customer may be offered lower prices than other customers if it costs the supplier less to service that customer, *and* if the supplier can prove this. Lower costs can result if the customer provides his own

FORM 7
COMPETITIVE OFFER INFORMATION FORM

(Give as much information as is available; if you requested information but it was not provided, write "not provided.")

1. Name of customer: _____
   Address: _____
2. Name of competitor: _____
3. Product(s) (be as specific as possible):
   _____

4. Nature of terms offered by competitor:
   (a) Price: _____
   (b) Quantity: _____
   (c) Other Terms: _____
   (d) Date of offer or sale: _____
   (e) Place of offer or sale: _____
   (f) Quoted by: _____
   (g) Quoted to: _____
   (h) Further details: (Furnish all information you have, attaching additional pages, if necessary; also, attach any documents, including documents obtained from the buyer, such as quotations or invoices.)
   _____
   _____
   _____

5. Information obtained:
   (a) From whom: _____
   (b) By whom: _____
   (c) When (Date and Time): _____
   (d) Where: _____
   (e) How (telephone, meeting, letter, etc.):
   _____
   _____

_____
Your Signature

_____
Your Title

_____
Date

means of delivery, for example, or purchases in such large lots that concrete, identifiable cost savings result. In practice, this is a difficult defense to establish successfully, and it should not be relied on without expert advice.

Other defenses include lowering prices in response to changing market conditions, as happens when part of a supplier's inventory becomes obsolete. Occasionally, a supplier also may try to demonstrate that the law should not apply because none of the transactions under scrutiny took place in interstate commerce, but this argument is rarely successful.

The Robinson-Patman Act has come under severe attack ever since its enactment on the ground that it actually stifles competition and consequently is at odds with the essential purpose of the antitrust laws. Calls for its repeal surface from time to time and government enforcement sometimes has been sporadic or virtually nonexistent. Nevertheless, this continues to be the law, and private parties continue to enforce it. Whenever suppliers discriminate in price, they should be on their guard. It is small comfort to companies that get sued to know that the Act has had so many detractors.

National Account Programs.

With so many retailers operating as part of regional or national chains today, a common marketing approach for suppliers has been the development of so-called "national account" programs. Typically, this involves a supplier arranging to sell to all, or at least many, of a retail group's outlets across the country, either directly or through independent wholesale distributors. Normally, a single, nationwide deal is struck to cover all of the outlets involved. Caution must be exercised in these situations to be sure that no unlawful discrimination is taking place, either in price or services, between the chain and other retailers who compete with it. In addition, if some or all of the sales will be made through independent wholesalers, there must be no resale price maintenance, even though the account may insist on only a single, nationwide price.

If the supplier finds it necessary to guarantee the price charged to the entire chain, he will have to make all the sales himself, with the wholesalers acting only as sales agents or consignees who never take title to the goods. Alternatively, the supplier can allow the wholesalers to make the sales themselves, but then each wholesaler should be given the option of selling at the national account price or at any other price he chooses. This may cause fragmentation, of course, and jeopardize the entire program. If the supplier has not granted each wholesaler an exclusive distributorship for each territory, however, the supplier can offer the national account price himself directly in those areas where the wholesaler chooses not to.

Customer restraints generally may be placed on wholesale distributors to preclude them from competing for national accounts reserved by the supplier. Suppliers usually can keep the distributors out of the national account arena and force them to concentrate their efforts on other categories of customers, stirring up more "interbrand" competition against other brands. Where the supplier is a monopolist, however (i.e., he is the only supplier of the relevant kind of product, or close to it), customer restrictions designed to reserve national accounts to the supplier may be susceptible to challenge under section 2 of the Sherman Act on the ground that there is little or no "interbrand" competition to begin with.

Note that suppliers ordinarily enlist the assistance of their distributors to service national accounts even where the supplier himself makes the sale and sets the price. This strategy ordinarily is lawful, so long as the supplier retains title to the goods until they are sold. Naturally, the distributors will expect to be compensated in some manner for their services.

Promotions.

Promotions normally are offers of special prices, services or other terms, which are extended for only a limited period of time. Suppliers may offer wholesalers or retailers promotions at certain times of the year or in periods of lagging sales in order to induce them to order more merchandise, and order it sooner. Promotions usually should be structured so that they are realistically available to the entire range of competing customers, or else alternative promotional materials should be made available. Introductions, however, are another story. The experience of Sterling Drug is illustrative.

CASE HISTORY: Luring Away Shelf Space.

Sterling Drug is the manufacturer of "Haley's M-O," which for years has been a leading over-the-counter laxative. To encourage wider distribution of this line, Sterling began to offer a year-long twenty-five percent discount to new customers who had not purchased or stocked M-O in any of its sizes within the preceding year. In effect, Sterling was offering a price incentive to new dealers for a one-year period, to persuade them to try placing M-O products on their shelves.

Interstate Cigar, a dealer which sold more than just cigars, already was carrying M-O. Shortly after Sterling's plan went into effect, Interstate bought large additional quantities of M-O, but it did not receive the lower price. When Interstate learned that a discount was being offered to new dealers—competitors of Interstate who had demonstrated no allegiance to the product in the past—it asked for the same price.

Sterling turned down this request on the ground that Interstate was not a new outlet, and therefore was ineligible to receive the discount. Interstate was outraged. It demanded to return part of its stock, and it sued. Who was right?

　　　1. Was Sterling required to offer the same discount to all dealers, both new and old? Was it permissible for Sterling to offer the discount to new dealers only, even though new dealers could be expected to compete with existing dealers?

　　　2. Could Sterling instead have offered a one-t·me allowance to any new dealers who agreed to take on its line, and afterward sell to them at its normal price? Would this have been any different in practical effect?

New dealer discounts, or "installation allowances," are fairly common in many industries. Although the old dealers may feel disadvantaged as long as the discount is in effect, this kind of incentive can be expected to increase competition in the long run rather than injure it, by encouraging the addition of more dealers. Often, the allowances are for opening orders only. Sterling's one-year arrangement may make more sense in certain industries, however, and Sterling won this case.

Credit Terms.

It is important to recognize that for some purposes (including price fixing) credit terms may be treated as an element of the price. When it comes to the Robinson-Patman Act, credit terms are normally taken into consideration, although they are not actually "prices," and are not really "services" provided in connection with resale either. Some courts, however, have taken the position that because the creditworthiness of each customer is a highly individualized matter, suppliers should be permitted the discretion to offer different terms to each customer. The supplier is bearing the risk of non-payment, and this makes the setting of credit terms considerably different from the setting of prices. But before offering different credit terms to different customers, a call to the legal department is in order, to make sure that the reasons for drawing these distinctions will stand up in court.

With all of these rules on collusion and discrimination going into the hopper, the determination of a selling price can be an agonizing experience. Yet for all the complexity, the legal tests are only the first hurdle. The real test of any pricing decision awaits in the marketplace, and the real trick is to arrive at a decision that makes both legal sense and business sense.

RESALE PRICES

One of life's great frustrations for manufacturers and other suppliers is that although they may have the power to determine the prices at which they sell to wholesalers or directly to retailers, subject to the rules described above, they do not have a direct voice over what the wholesalers can charge the retailers or what the retailers can charge the public. Suppliers naturally would like to see their products sold to the public at retail prices which will maximize the suppliers' own profits. They also want their dealers to earn enough revenue to encourage them to push the products enthusiastically. We already have seen that resale price maintenance is *per se* unlawful. We have also seen that there are various non-price restrictions which can be imposed upon dealers in order to provide similar incentives. Beyond that, there are also several specific pricing practices in which suppliers may engage to influence resale prices, other than resale price maintenance, and these can be entirely lawful. The most important are described below.

Suggesting Resale Prices.

Suggesting resale prices historically has been among the safest means of influencing prices at subsequent levels of distribution. Numerous cases have upheld the principle that it is not illegal for a supplier to suggest resale prices to his dealers. Today, suggested resale prices are common in an enormous number of industries, for products ranging from automobiles to electronics to cosmetics.

Suggested prices are no more than guidelines for wholesalers and retailers. In the case of new products, suggested prices may serve the important purpose of helping dealers to position an untried commodity. The supplier may have undertaken a market study in advance and developed information on optimal pricing. In the case of fledgling dealers, suggested prices may help them to begin marketing even established products, since they may not immediately know what to charge for every item in their inventories.

There must be no compulsion to adhere to suggested price lists, of course, and dealers must remain free to charge more or less than the suggested figures. Naturally, if the supplier operates some retail outlets himself, he will normally offer his products at the suggested prices at those locations, and this may set something of an example. Suggested retail prices also may be preprinted on packaging by the supplier, and included in the supplier's advertising, so long as independent retailers retain their discretion to charge other prices.

"Participating Dealer" Offers.

It has become increasingly common for suppliers to advertise price promotions "at participating dealers." Some suppliers badly want to be able to advertise prices, particularly during promotions, but at the same time they do not want to be guilty of collusion over pricing. This can present something of a challenge.

So long as promotions are limited to participating dealers only, other dealers remain free not to participate and to sell on whatever terms they choose. In reality, of course, the dealers may be under substantial pressure from consumers to participate. If they don't, the dealers risk disappointing consumers who arrive expecting to pay the promotion price, and those consumers may be permanently alienated. At the same time, if many dealers refuse to participate, this may seal the doom of a promotional program entirely. Suppliers cannot continue for long to advertise a program which a large percentage of their dealers do not support. (If the dealers band together and *agree* not to participate, however, they may be flirting with an antitrust violation themselves.)

A variation of the "participating dealer" type of program is to advertise that all participating dealers will be offering "ten dollars off" or "ten percent off" their regular price for some period. This permits each dealer to determine his own regular price prior to the promotion, and even if all participate, the program will not require price uniformity. A program like this is less vulnerable to attack as resale price fixing.

The most important thing to remember in any of these programs is to insure that the dealers really retain the discretion to charge whatever price they choose. Most or all of them may choose to participate, particularly in the case of an attractive, well-designed and well-publicized program, but they must have a genuine option to refuse.

Consignments.

Another mechanism by which a supplier can influence prices at succeeding levels of distribution is by selling on consignment. This approach is not always practical, but when it is, the supplier's control over prices is complete.

For many years it was generally accepted that consignment sales provided a perfectly effective and lawful alternative approach to distribution, which enabled the supplier to set retail prices since the supplier actually owned the goods until the moment they were sold to the consumer. The principal drawback, of course, was that the supplier had to finance and insure the inventories consigned to each of his dealers, but many suppliers were willing to bear that burden. In 1964, the Supreme Court struck down one consignment scheme as a sham, on the ground that the risk of loss had substantially shifted to the dealer, and the supplier's intention was simply to fix prices.* After that, many observers concluded that, as a practical matter, consignments would no longer be recognized as a viable basis on which to control retail prices.

A number of suppliers abandoned consignment in favor of other arrangements at that time, but the predictions of the demise of consignment sales were premature. Subsequent decisions permitted consignors, including consignors of such diverse products as gasoline, baked goods and rental trailers, to set retail prices so long as the consignments were "legitimate." These cases have continued to recognize the right of a consignor to determine the prices at which his goods will be sold through

---

Simpson v. Union Oil Co.

his consignees, provided that certain conditions are satisfied: (1) The consignment plan must not be a sham set up principally to facilitate price fixing; (2) the supplier must retain title and risk of loss; and (3) the consignee must be performing, essentially, in the same manner as an employee.

The rule permitting "legitimate" consignors to set retail prices makes economic sense. There is no question that a "vertically integrated" supplier—one who actually owns and operates his own retail outlets—is entitled to set the retail prices for his goods. By the same reasoning, a supplier who, under a consignment plan, is called upon to finance an inventory and assume the risk of loss, damage and sluggish sales, should also have the right to control the retail marketing strategy, including determination of retail prices. This still is not to say that a supplier may switch to a fake "consignment" arrangement for the very purpose of fixing prices, but where appropriate, a legitimate consignment plan can be implemented and retail prices can be set.

Switching over to a consignment plan, however, is not necessarily a piece of cake. While the dealers may welcome a consignment plan because they will no longer have to finance their inventory, they may not be happy about losing control over their pricing or their profit margins. Not long ago, Porsche, the German automaker, decided to switch its entire distribution network in the United States over to a consignment arrangement. Reportedly unhappy with complaints about dealer service and the high mark-ups which some dealers were taking on popular models, Porsche decided to terminate all of its existing dealers and sell directly to consumers. It planned to continue delivering the cars through some of the same dealerships it already had, but it would use the dealers only as agents, who reportedly would be paid a flat eight percent fee for their services. Porsche did not reckon with the irate response it encountered from its dealers, however, or with the federal Dealer Day in Court Act, which proscribes termination of automobile dealers without good cause. Threatened with massive litigation, Porsche quickly retreated, abandoning the entire plan.

Rebates.

One of the most popular methods for influencing resale prices in recent years has been the use of the rebate. Once confined largely to costly goods such as automobiles, rebate offers have appeared lately for such items as toasters, smoke detectors and light bulbs. The advantage of rebates is that the manufacturer deals directly with the consumer, limiting the chances for unlawful conspiracies with the dealers to arise, and limiting the dealers' opportunity to pocket the savings themselves. The disadvantage, which may not matter to some suppliers, is that rebates can be used only to lower the effective retail price, not to curtail discounting. They also may be costly to administer.

Often, rebates are applied to articles which have a manufacturer's suggested retail price. For example, in the auto industry, vehicles are required under federal law to carry stickers bearing their manufacturer's suggested list price. From this can be deducted any additional discount which the retailer may choose, and any rebate which the manufacturer may offer. Rebates have been especially popular in moving large inventories at the end of a model year or disposing of less popular models. In other industries, such as small appliances, rebates have been used in lieu of price reductions to combat consumer resistance to high prices. A typical advertisement for an appliance might read:

Mfr's Suggested Retail:	$25.00
Retailer's Price:	20.00
Mfr's Rebate:	5.00
You Pay Only:	$15.00

Rebates permit the supplier to lower effective retail prices without lowering either his own prices to dealers or his suggested retail prices. This has two effects. First, it largely eliminates the possibility that dealers will fail to pass the savings along to their customers, which could occur if the supplier simply lowers his own prices instead. The rebate is paid directly to the consumer, and the dealers cannot profit from it except in the rare case where it encourages them to raise their own prices.

Second, rebates may facilitate the understatement of any future price increases. For example, if a supplier offers a thousand dollar rebate on an eight thousand dollar model (suggested retail price) at the end of the first model year, and then raises the price by a thousand dollars in the second year, *and* eliminates the rebate, the supplier's press release may report a price increase of twelve and a half percent, but the effective increase actually will be over twenty-eight percent.

Rebates have been the subject of very little antitrust litigation, and when scrutinized, they normally have not been found to constitute price fixing. The key feature of the rebate in this regard is that it should not require the retailer to charge any particular price. In practical effect, some retailers may adhere to suggested prices during a rebate program on the theory that consumers are already receiving enough of a price break to encourage them to buy. Other retailers may seize upon rebate programs to add special discounts of their own. The retailer may want to promote such offers vigorously, especially if there is cooperative advertising available.

The possibility usually is remote that retailers will take advantage of a rebate program to raise their prices on the theory that consumers will make up for the increase and more in the form of the rebate. If the items are so popular that the retailer can raise his prices, particularly above the suggested retail prices, the manufacturer is not likely to institute a rebate program in the first place.

There are other legal considerations which must be taken into account, however. If the dealers are required to contribute to a rebate program, this fact may have to be disclosed in advertising, at least where the price of the product normally is the subject of bargaining, as with automobiles. Any preconditions for payment of a rebate must be disclosed in advance, and they must be reasonable. Also, anyone offering a rebate must take steps to ensure that adequate systems are in place to process requests for rebates promptly. And if rebate payments are promised within a certain period of time, those promises must be kept. Otherwise, enforcement actions may be initiated by the Federal Trade Commission or state consumer protection bureaus.

Coupons.

Coupons are another phenomenon which also permit the supplier to provide a discount directly to the consumer. As noted earlier, when suppliers offer price promotions to dealers there often is no guarantee that those savings will be passed along to consumers. Dealers may simply take the opportunity to stock up at low cost without offering consumers the same break, frustrating the supplier's plan. Coupons have no effect on the shelf prices of each retailer, but they do assure the consumer of receiving a set discount off those prices (or more, if the retailer chooses to offer "double coupons" or similar programs).

The principal shortcoming of coupons, of course, is that they do not reach all potential consumers. Only those consumers who actually receive the coupons can participate. Also, there are substantial costs involved, for targeting and mailing as well as for redemption. The advantage, aside from assuring that the consumer realizes a savings, is that coupons do not provide a basis for allegations of price fixing. They permit the supplier to provide consumers with reduced prices without interfering with the dealers' pricing discretion at all. This advantage, in itself, may not be sufficient reason to initiate a coupon program, but if coupons are otherwise appropriate to a marketing plan, they can offer the supplier the added bonus of eliminating a multitude of legal hazards.

Sales Assistance Programs.

Promotional allowances, or dealer assistance programs, have become increasingly popular in recent years. Suppliers frequently reduce their prices to dealers to enable the dealers to offer lower prices to consumers. Usually this is done in connection with a special promotional program or to meet competitive pressure from other brands. Where the purpose is to meet competition, the allowances may be provided to dealers on a dealer-by-dealer basis. Where the allowances are part of a broad scale promotional effort, all the dealers who compete with one another in the same area should be included, to avoid charges of price discrimination.

The more difficult question is whether the supplier may require each dealer to lower his own prices to the public as a condition of receiving the special prices from the supplier. Until recently, there was substantial concern that such a requirement would constitute illegal resale price maintenance, because the supplier would be influencing what the dealer could charge. Today, the law has come around to the view that if the supplier is willing to lower his price to the dealer, he is entitled to some expectation that the dealer will pass along the savings to the customer. If a sales assistance program turns out to be a sham, intended simply to maintain resale prices, it may still be considered illegal. But well-intended dealer assistance programs are likely to pass muster. The recent experience of Mack Trucks provides a good illustration:

CASE HISTORY: Persuasion on Prices.

Even if your product is "built like a Mack truck," the delicate subject of retail prices can still be a concern. Mack Trucks sold its vehicles through independent dealers, each of whom was free to determine his own retail prices. But Mack was concerned about price competition from other brands, and wanting to sell more trucks, it instituted a "sales assistance program" to insure that its line would remain competitive.

Under this plan, Mack effectively lowered its prices to dealers who were having trouble meeting competitive offers. In return, however, Mack required that the dealers actually pass along the savings to their customers.

To receive assistance, a dealer had to submit an application to Mack, specifying the price he estimated he would have to charge in order to make the sale. The dealer also was required to describe the nature of the competition which made the lower price necessary.

If Mack approved, it would agree to lower its wholesale price to the dealer by an amount that would guarantee the dealer a specified minimum profit (usually 4 percent of list price). After the dealer actually landed the order, Mack would manufacture the truck to order and sell it to the dealer at its ordinary wholesale price. The dealer would then resell the truck to his customer, and report the final sales price to Mack. If, as anticipated, the dealer had not realized the minimum profit level on the sale, Mack reduced its own wholesale price by the appropriate amount and credited the dealer's account with the difference. If it turned out that the dealer's profit unexpectedly exceeded the anticipated amount, Mack granted no sales assistance, or reduced the price only to the extent necessary to allow the dealer the guaranteed profit.

One dealer, Lewis, became unhappy with the program. Lewis contended that Mack really was dictating retail prices by keeping its wholesale prices so high that Lewis was being forced to resort to the sales assistance program more often than not. As a consequence, in more than half of his sales, Lewis was effectively limited to a 4 percent profit margin. Once Mack would agree to lower its wholesale price, Lewis would no longer be in a position to negotiate with his customer over price, because even if he could get a few dollars more at that stage, any added revenue automatically would be offset by a reduction in the assistance from Mack.

Mack, for its part, took the position that it had a right to insist that any discount it provided would be passed along to the customer, and not pocketed by the dealer. To put it another way, Mack felt that if it was willing to reduce its own profit in order to assist the dealer to make a sale, the dealer should be satisfied with a lower profit as well.

But Lewis insisted that his prices were being fixed and the matter was litigated, raising several questions:

1. Was Mack telling Lewis what to charge? What kind of flexibility was Mack denying to Lewis? How different was the sales assistance program from outright resale price fixing?

2. How was Lewis hurt? Could Mack have accomplished the same thing through a rebate program? Could Mack have sold

directly to fleet operators and other large customers, choosing
whatever price it saw fit to charge?

Making sure that price reductions filter down to the consumer
has been a serious concern of many suppliers. Several courts
recently have adopted the view that these concerns are legitimate, and the efforts of a number of suppliers to require that
discounts be passed along by their dealers have been looked
upon with favor. This included Mack, which won its case with
Lewis. So long as the retail prices charged by the dealers are not
being fixed, efforts by suppliers to help their dealers lower those
prices ordinarily will be upheld.

Sales Incentives.

Another approach to influencing resale prices involves
sales incentives aimed directly at the dealers' personnel. Even
if the dealers are not realizing a sufficient return to encourage
them to promote the supplier's products vigorously, incentives
can be applied directly in the form of such devices as direct commissions and sales contests.

For example, the supplier of a new line of appliances may
decide that retailers cannot be relied upon to push his products
adequately. The supplier could suggest a relatively large mark-
up and hope that the retailers take it and devote a substantial
part of their margins to promotion. Instead, the supplier may
choose to spur sales efforts more directly by offering to pay a
ten percent commission directly to the sales personnel employed by each retailer. As an extra incentive, the supplier may
offer to give each of the top five grossers of the year nationwide
a free trip for two to Tahiti.

At the time the program is introduced, the supplier may
also help build consumer demand by providing special displays
and demonstrators. In this way the supplier may be able to generate nearly the same sales effort as he could through resale
price maintenance, without raising the spectre of conspiracy.

Commissions and other incentives of this kind must be disclosed to the retailer in advance. Also, caution must be exercised

to avoid problems under the Robinson-Patman Act, and incentives should normally be offered to all retailers on a proportionally equal basis.

In the end, getting the product to market at the right retail price without sacrificing any other element of a marketing plan is no easy undertaking. Choosing the supplier's selling price and influencing resale prices along the line of distribution is a tough challenge from a legal perspective as well as a business perspective—and there are few business decisions in which the law has taken so keen an interest.

Six

ADVERTISING AND SELLING

Once a distribution network has been established and the supplier determines how much to charge for his products, customers have to be convinced to buy them. Advertising programs and sales calls raise a host of legal issues, and an ounce of prevention may well be worth a pound of litigation down the road. Promotional programs run in cooperation with dealers must be administered fairly. Advertising and sales presentations may be zealous, but they may not be deceptive or unfair.

COOPERATIVE ADVERTISING PLACED BY THE SUPPLIER

Some suppliers organize cooperative advertising programs under which their dealers are required to make contributions, often based on a percentage of sales, to an advertising fund administered by the supplier. This is particularly common in the field of franchising. The supplier typically uses the advertising fund to pay for area-wide or nationwide advertising to promote the brand on a broad scale. This permits use of media such as television and national magazines which might not be practical for any single dealer.

Suppliers, however, must be careful to treat their dealers equitably, and not to use this kind of advertising in an anticompetitive manner. The advertising should not favor one dealer's interests over another, either by featuring only certain dealers' facilities or in any other manner. If the supplier operates some of the dealerships himself, these should not be favored either.

Is it lawful to require dealers to contribute to advertising funds in the first place? Those courts that have addressed the question have held that such a practice is permissible. Franchise organizations, including such groups as transmission repair chains and hotel chains, have regularly required franchisees to contribute to funds used to place national or regional advertising. Usually it is in the interest of all the dealers to have awareness of the brand strengthened across the country.

ADVERTISING ALLOWANCES

Advertising allowances are payments made by a supplier to his dealers to assist them in placing advertising themselves, or to reimburse them for advertising which they have already placed. Advertising allowances are often characterized simply as a form of cooperative advertising. They are widely used, and exist in an almost endless number of varieties. But bear in mind that they must be offered in a nondiscriminatory manner when competing dealers are involved (except to meet competition), since they are subject to the Robinson-Patman Act.

Specifically, when a supplier offers advertising allowances, he should make them available on proportionally equal terms to all of his dealers who compete with one another. This can be accomplished simply by basing the amount of payments on each dealer's volume, but any other method which is fair to all the dealers will also be acceptable.

The supplier should employ some measures to inform all competing dealers of the existence and nature of the allowance plan, so that they all may take advantage of it. Notice can be given by sending the dealers the terms of the plan, or at least a general summary of it accompanied by an explanation of how to get additional details. Notification of new programs also can be given on a continuing basis by, among other things, publishing announcements in trade journals.

Promotional allowances do not have to be offered to every dealer in the country, but only to dealers who compete with one another in the same trade area. If certain trade areas, such as metropolitan areas, are isolated from one another, it may be possible to offer an allowance program only to the dealers in selected areas. Care should be taken, however, not to discriminate against dealers on the fringe of an apparent trade area, if those dealers are actually in competition with the dealers inside that area.

The plan must be structured so that all competing dealers in areas where the plan operates are able to participate, or that, if some are not in a position to participate, suitable alternatives will be offered. For example, if elaborate display materials are provided for major department stores, smaller retailers will be furnished with promotional services on a smaller scale which they can use.

The supplier also should make sure that the dealers receiving the allowances actually are placing the advertising. If the supplier knows or has reason to believe that a dealer is keeping the advertising allowance and not placing the advertising, the payments should be discontinued. The supplier should require evidence whenever possible, showing that the advertising has been placed, such as tear sheets or copies of invoices from radio stations.

Where the supplier sells to wholesalers who resell the product to retailers, the supplier still may provide advertising allowances to retailers by working through the wholesalers. As with direct programs, however, the supplier should afford all the retailers proportionally equal treatment, give adequate notice to the retailers involved, insure that the plan is functionally available to all competing retailers, and check that the retailers are actually placing the advertising.

As with price discrimination, customers who knowingly induce advertising allowances or other promotional services that are not available on proportionally equal terms to competing dealers may be violating the law. The same holds true for inducing services provided by brokers or other outside firms acting on behalf of the supplier. Also, the retailer should only be keeping advertising allowances which fairly reflect the costs of the advertising which he has placed. If the retailer subsequently receives any rebate or other reimbursement from the media, these amounts should be refunded to the supplier. In fact, broadcasters and publishers themselves may run into legal trouble if they provide dealers with misleading invoices or rate schedules that do not reflect discounts or rebates which the dealers have earned.

The "meeting competition" defense discussed in the preceding chapter applies as well to advertising allowances and other promotional services. A supplier is entitled to provide discriminatory advertising allowances or other promotional payments to dealers if this is done in order to meet competition from another supplier. The "cost justification" defense, however, only applies to price discrimination, and does not extend to discrimination in the payment of advertising allowances or furnishing promotional services.

The controlling principle for suppliers here is to treat all dealers equitably, in order to avoid charges of unlawful discrimination. Advertising allowances are fine, but they cannot be used as a vehicle to reward favored dealers. Often the dealers know how to advertise on their local turf better than anyone else, but if the supplier wants to encourage such activity on the part of any of his dealers in a marketing area, he must provide the same opportunity to all of them, unless he is meeting competition. Despite this limitation, some flexibility is still retained because, as noted above, the supplier can make different arrangements in each geographic area.

AVOIDING DECEPTIVE ADVERTISING

Advertising may beguile, but it may not mislead. False and deceptive advertising has long been a concern of the law, and as advertising claims have become more sophisticated, so have the legal standards. Although the legal concerns may be shouldered in some measure by the advertising agencies and their lawyers, advertisers themselves must assume responsibility for insuring the honesty of their ads, and marketing executives should at least know the basics of what the law demands before they take the first steps in initiating an advertising campaign.

Each advertising case is unique, but certain basic legal principles govern advertising. The problems encountered by Tropicana's advertising a few years ago illustrate the type of conflict that may arise and the principles that apply.

CASE HISTORY: Oranges' Origins.

Tropicana Products, the well-known orange juice producer, aired a television commercial not long ago featuring Olympic decathlon champion Bruce Jenner squeezing the juice out of an orange and into an open Tropicana "Premium Pack" container. Said Mr. Jenner:

> Tropicana Premium Pack. For me, it tastes freshest. It's pure pasteurized juice as it comes from the orange. It's the only leading brand not made with concentrate and water.

This pitch made The Coca-Cola Company, maker of Minute Maid orange juice, see red. Minute Maid itself was, in fact, produced by using concentrate and water. But Tropicana was not exactly made by squeezing oranges directly into paper cartons.

Actually, Tropicana Premium Pack orange juice was made by a rather unique process which involved pasteurizing the juice prior to packaging, by heating it to about 200° Fahrenheit. Following pasteurization, the juice was sometimes frozen in bulk for some period and later thawed and packaged as needed. It was never concentrated, however.

As Coca-Cola saw it, the Tropicana commercial was misleading because it gave the impression that the Premium Pack carton contained unprocessed, fresh-squeezed juice, when in fact the juice had been heated and may also have been frozen prior to packaging. Also, the phrase "pure pasteurized juice as it comes from the orange" was itself something of an anomaly, since no oranges on the tree ever contain pasteurized juice. Tropicana contended that inclusion of the word "pasteurized" eliminated any possibility of deception, because it is common knowledge that pasteurization requires heating, and no one listening to the commercial could hear that the juice was pasteurized and still believe that it was squeezed directly into the container. Coca-Cola, on the other hand, argued that the phrase "pasteurized juice as it comes from the orange" was simply false and deceptive. The dispute wound up in court, raising some fascinating questions:

1. Was the commercial deceptive? If so, how could it have been revised to make it non-deceptive and still get the message across?

2. Could Coca-Cola have proved deception by commissioning a consumer survey? What kind of survey would have been suitable?

3. What remedies are available in cases like this?

Deception is often in the eye of the beholder, and in a case like this it is not surprising to find the trial level judge reaching one conclusion, while the appellate court reaches the opposite conclusion. That is what happened, with the trial level court refusing to issue a preliminary injunction against Tropicana, and the appellate court reversing and ordering that the preliminary injunction·be entered. Ultimately, the litigation was settled.

Consumer surveys are usually valuable in cases like this, except in the most blatant situations where they are unnecessary. But it is certain that the methodology behind any survey will be subjected to the closest scrutiny in court. Coca-Cola introduced a consumer survey in this case which measured the impact of Tropicana's commercial. Tropicana was able to demonstrate that the methodology of the survey was flawed, because it focused on what was seen more than on what was heard.

The FTC Guidelines.

Space does not permit an exhaustive catalogue of all the specific kinds of representations which have been judged deceptive in decided cases, but the Federal Trade Commission, which has primary responsibility for policing deceptive advertising, has established certain guidelines. Not surprisingly, these guidelines are subject to change from time to time as the composition of the Commission itself changes. For this reason, it is useful to have the latest advice on the state of the law before committing to any new advertising program.

The practice of the FTC is to focus on the overall impression an ad makes on the public. Even if an advertisement is not literally false, the Commission also can consider the implications of its words, pictures and other elements in determining whether it should be challenged as deceptive. To take an example, one manufacturer some years ago made the claim that his product gave "quick relief from itching of eczema." The product was, in fact, effective in relieving itching, but it was totally ineffective in remedying eczema. Although the statement only claimed to relieve the itching, the Commission concluded that the ad falsely gave the general impression that the product also remedied the disease itself.

There has been some debate over the past few years as to whether the applicable standard should be the impression an advertisement makes on consumers who act "reasonably," or the impression made even on consumers who act casually or inattentively. Recently, the Commission announced that its policy will be to protect against deception only of consumers who interpret the advertisement reasonably in the circumstances, and are likely to be injured by the misleading message. Often, this distinction will make no difference, but in close cases it may, and it is important to keep abreast of developments in this area if your own advertisements could be affected.

The Commission is not required to produce proof of actual deception in order to halt an advertising program, and a likelihood of deception will suffice. For example, the makers of Geritol in years past advertised that "if you are often tired and run down, you will feel stronger fast by taking Geritol." The FTC complained that the advertisement was deceptive because the product was only effective in relieving iron deficiency, which was only one cause of fatigue. In challenging the advertisement, the Commission was not required to document instances of actual deception, since the facts demonstrated that a likelihood of deception existed. Also, the magnitude of deception does not have to be overwhelming. In one case, a court concluded that the deception of fewer than fifteen percent of the people polled sufficed as the basis for enforcement.

In some instances the Commission can establish that an advertiser has committed deception by silence, since a half-truth sometimes can be as deceptive as a positive misrepresentation. The most difficult issue in such cases is to determine when a piece of information is so relevant that the advertiser is obliged to disclose it. In order to require disclosure of a fact, the Commission must be able to demonstrate that anything negative which would be revealed by the fact is a material consequence of normal use of the product, yet is something that is not generally known or expected. For example, a drug manufacturer could be required to disclose material and relatively common side effects of a drug product. Also, the Commission may require disclosure of additional facts on the ground that they are necessary to dissipate some false assumption which an advertisement is likely to create. Advertisers of baldness remedies, for example, were required in the past to disclose that most baldness is hereditary and largely untreatable. (More recently, steps have been taken by the Food and Drug Administration to have these products removed from the market entirely.)

When introducing a new product, it is also important to make sure that the advertising for the product is accurate at the time it is run. Several computer manufacturers ran into trouble recently by claiming that their hardware was capable of performing certain functions which were not yet possible because the necessary software was not ready at the time the claims were made. (This practice had become sufficiently prevalent for the cognoscenti to have coined the term "vaporware" to describe the nonexistent software.) The fact that the software did become available later on did not change the fact that the ads were considered deceptive as of the time the performance claims originally were made.

Some advertisements may be susceptible of both a misleading and a truthful interpretation at the same time, and these can also be considered deceptive. In one case an ad for floor wax represented that the wax would last for six months. The Commission complained that this was misleading because while the wax lasted six months, it became terribly dirty and scuffed. The manufacturer responded that the representation merely claimed that the wax would remain on the floor for six months, which it did. A court upheld the Commission on this one, finding that there was a misleading interpretation to be drawn from the ad as well, and this caused it to be deceptive.

It should be noted that deceptive advertising cannot be cured by offering money-back guarantees or warranties. The Commission will not allow a seller to advertise a non-waterproof watch as waterproof, for example, simply because the seller is willing to replace any watches which are ruined by water. Some marketers try to rely on their guarantees to excuse their deceptive claims, but the Commission will not permit this.

It is also important to point out that a representation can be so obviously inflated that it cannot possibly be considered deceptive. Highly exaggerated claims for a product often will be held to be nothing more than harmless "puffery" if the assertion is not really capable of creating any false or misleading impression. A toothpaste manufacturer once claimed that its product would give users "the smile of beauty." The Commission looked at the claim and concluded that it was not deceptive because it was so general and could have so many meanings. Words like "amazing" also have been held to be mere puffing, and not taken literally by the public.

In certain cases, the Commission may proceed against an advertising campaign that is not, strictly speaking, deceptive, on the ground that for some reason it is nevertheless "unfair." This is particularly true in the case of advertising claims made without adequate prior substantiation, even if they turn out to be true. The Commission has taken the position that advertisers must undertake to substantiate their claims before they present them to the public. Substantiation generated after the claim is made cannot be counted on, even if the facts happen to support the claim. The Commission may decide not to take action on the basis of such subsequent substantiation in particular cases, but this is a matter of discretion.

The Commission has provided some concrete indications of its enforcement intentions with regard to ad substantiation. It will require relatively higher levels of substantiation for claims regarding health, safety and the effectiveness of products; for claims involving foods, drugs and potentially hazardous products; for claims which, if false, might cause injury or property damage; for the kinds of claims on which consumers are particulary likely to rely; and for claims of the types which are most easily substantiated. In targeting advertisements to scrutinize for adequate substantiation, the Commission also has been especially concerned with overbroad claims which are sometimes true, but only under certain unspecified conditions. An example of this was a gasoline additive advertised as eliminating all exhaust emissions in all cars, which really only reduced some emissions in some cars.

In addition, the Commission has issued Guides concerning the use of endorsements in advertising. These require, among other things, that any statements made by the endorser reflect the endorser's honestly held belief and be capable of substantiation. Also, endorsements by consumers should reflect typical consumer experience with the product.

The Commission is more likely to target advertisers who place large numbers of ads, since proceeding against these advertisers is likely to have the greatest impact on advertising generally. If violations are particularly widespread, the Commission has sometimes chosen to develop industry-wide trade rules instead of concerning itself with individual offenders. Such rules exist in the funeral industry and the home insulation industry, to name but two.

In addition, the Commission is more likely to move against an advertiser whose claims affect a vulnerable group such as children or the elderly. But the Commission is less likely to become involved in matters which can be corrected by market forces. For example, if an item is of low cost and consumers can determine prior to purchase or with limited experience with the product that the claims are baseless, the Commission may be somewhat less likely to investigate the claim's substantiation.

Remedies.

Traditionally, the FTC has been afforded broad discretion in choosing remedies with which to counter deceptive and unfair practices. Most commonly, the Commission issues an order which requires the advertiser to discontinue the offending ad. Violations of such orders can carry civil penalties of up to ten thousand dollars for each offense. Where appropriate, the Commission also may issue an order requiring the disclosure of material facts.

One of the most radical remedies, however, is to require corrective advertising. The Commission's power to order corrective advertising has been upheld where a deceptive ad has substantially created a false belief in the public's mind which persists even after the advertising ceases. The leading case involved Listerine mouthwash advertisements. The Commission found that these ads had created a false belief that the product was capable of preventing and curing colds and sore throats. It concluded that this false belief would linger on after the offending advertisement had ceased running, and ordered Listerine to include a disclaimer in every future advertisement over a specified period of time.

Of course, the First Amendment guarantees free speech, and this includes commercial "speech" on behalf of businesses. The First Amendment prevents the Commission from imposing any remedy which is broader than necessary to prevent deception or correct its effects. For example, an FTC order which prohibited a loan company from using the slogan "instant tax refund," because the loans it offered bore no relationship to such refunds, was found to exceed the Commission's authority. In another case, the Commission was unsuccessful in an attempt to require an egg industry trade association to include a statement in future ads to the effect that many medical experts believe that egg consumption increases the risk of heart disease.

As these examples illustrate, the Commission's discretion to fashion remedies is not unlimited. At the same time, advertisers should not forget that corrective advertising still may be imposed if an ad creates a false impression which persists after the advertising has been withdrawn.

The Commission is not the only enforcement body with an interest in advertising. The Food and Drug Administration has jurisdiction over the advertising of foods, drugs and cosmetics, which it shares with the FTC. Increasingly, state and local consumer protection offices as well as the United States Postal Service also have become active, and any one of these agencies may proceed against advertisements even if the Commission chooses not to act.

In addition, private parties can commence proceedings, just as Coca-Cola did against Tropicana. Aggrieved competitors may sue for unfair competition, or for violations of a certain section of the federal trademark laws, known as section 43(a) of the Lanham Act. This section provides for private suits by anyone who is damaged by false descriptions or representations used in connection with goods sold in interstate commerce. Injured competitors also may initiate hearings before the National Advertising Division of the Council of Better Business Bureaus. Consumers may be entitled to sue in certain circumstances as well, for consumer fraud or under some state "little FTC Acts." The best defense for the advertiser in all types of cases, of course, is advertising which tells the truth.

SALESMANSHIP AND THE LAW

Aggressive salesmanship is not a crime, but there are limits beyond which sales representatives can run into trouble. Lying about your own product, maligning your competitors or their products, and threatening your customers are indiscretions of the type the law usually will not countenance. Much of this kind of conduct is governed by state law on unfair competition, most of which is not spelled out in statutes but has evolved through thousands of cases over the years. In addition, improper sales tactics may provide evidence of antitrust violations or other law-breaking.

In selling a product, as in advertising, mere "puffery" has always been permitted. Sales representatives can tell customers that their product is "terrific," since everyone knows how little comments like this are worth. Problems develop, however, when more specific claims are made which cannot be substantiated, since customers are more likely to place reliance on them. Misrepresenting one's product is not fair play, and if it injures a competitor or a customer, it may not be legal either. It is also illegal to "pass off" your product as that of another supplier, and tales of counterfeit watches, clothing and other items being passed off as the genuine article have become commonplace. More subtle techniques which mislead a buyer into believing that he is purchasing one brand of a product when he is actually purchasing another can amount to illegal passing off as well.

Comparisons can also spell trouble if not well supervised. Comparing one's product with the competition can be a very dramatic sales technique—if your product is superior. When a comparison is presented fairly, it is entirely acceptable and represents the very essence of competition. It is fine for a sales representative to tell a customer that his products offer higher quality, better performance, faster delivery and greater reliability than his competitors' products—if these claims can be substantiated. This is generally safer, and usually more effective, than insisting that the other guy's products are inferior. Most successful suits over product claims involve allegations of maligning competitors' products. It is much harder to make out a claim of unfair competition by demonstrating only that a firm extolled the virtues of its own products.

Of course, there are other unacceptable practices which sales representatives have been known to engage in, generally classified as "dirty tricks." One example involved a quick-fingered salesman of coated photocopy paper who landed his company in court some years ago. His technique was to visit potential customers who were using a competitor's paper and run off a good quality copy on the customer's machine, using his own company's paper. Then he would switch to the competitor's paper, but while changing the paper he also would change the shutter setting of the machine so that it could not run off a satisfactory copy on any paper. He would then make an inferior copy on his competitor's paper, and—you guessed it—blame it on the paper.

Other "dirty tricks" have been no less devious. These include such grim tactics as theft of secret customer lists and other trade secrets, bribing purchasing agents, falsely telling customers that a competitor is going out of business to induce them to break contracts, and even sabotaging a competitor's facilities. Much of this activity, of course, is also criminal. All of it is likely to give rise to charges of unfair competition and, if the perpetrator is large enough, attempted monopolization.

Another type of improper technique—sometimes called *reverse* passing off—is displaying your competitor's product as your own, to conceal the fact that your own product is not available yet or is just not as good. In one case, an electronics supplier displayed a Panasonic portable radio at the Consumer Electronics Show with his own logo on it, in order to solicit sales for his own product, which was not yet on hand. In another case, a supplier actually submitted samples of his competitor's ventilation equipment to potential customers for evaluation, without disclosing whose it was, or that he was not yet prepared to make the same product himself. Just as it is illegal to pass off your product as that of another, it is equally illegal to pass off a competitor's product as your own in order to deceive customers and gain a competitive advantage. It is entirely proper, on the other hand, to display mock-ups to customers of products that are about to go into production, even though production models are not yet available. What you cannot do is use your competitor's product as a selling prop to create a false impression that this is your product, that your product is this good, and your product is available now.

An entirely different problem associated with selling is heavy-handedness in dealing with customers, including dealers. Tensions between suppliers and dealers already have been explored at length in this volume, but it is usually the supplier's sales contingent that bears the brunt of this ill will, and some-times helps to create it. Sales representatives normally are per-mitted to use strong persuasion to urge dealers to buy their company's product, or to buy more of it, or not to buy so much of somebody else's product. Sales representatives are, after all, supposed to sell. What they should not do is take it upon them-selves to threaten dealers with termination or other conse-quences for failing to accede to their demands. If they are displeased with a dealer's performance, purchasing habits or level of cooperation, they should report this up the line. Deci-sions to discipline or terminate a dealer should await the ap-proval of management and the lawyers.

At the retail level, a number of disfavored selling tactics, such as "bait and switch," deceptive pricing, and deceptive use of the word "free," are covered by specific Federal Trade Com-mission Guides. The Commission has also issued trade regu-lation rules which regulate door-to-door sales, mail order sales, food store advertising practices and games of chance in food outlets and service stations. Retailers and their lawyers should be conversant with any of these provisions which apply to them, and suppliers should at least be aware of the rules under which retailers operate in their industry.

Selling is an art, as is advertising, and artists must be per-mitted to do their work. On the other hand, this is one area in which "artistic license" has its limits. (See the list of "cautions" on pages 131-132.) Urging, demonstrating and convincing are the very tools of competition. Lying, maligning and strong-arm-ing are not. Sales representatives must be carefully briefed be-fore being dispatched into the field, to make certain that while they are out there selling your products, they are not also buy-ing you lawsuits.

CAUTIONS FOR SALES REPRESENTATIVES

1. Don't make claims about your products that have not been substantiated. Know the facts in advance.

2. Don't make claims about competing products that have not been substantiated. Don't knock the quality or performance of competing goods unless you already know that your company has available valid test results or other proof to back you up.

3. Don't make claims about your competitors' ability to perform, or about their financial conduction, unless you have proof that these claims are true. Don't criticize your competitors' ability to deliver on time or provide service unless you have hard evidence.

4. Don't pretend that a sample of your competitor's product is your own company's product, just because you haven't got any samples of your own merchandise yet, or yours is not as well made.

5. Don't misrepresent who manufactured the products you are selling, or what brand they are.

6. Don't try to obtain customer lists or other trade secrets from your competitors through bribery, theft or other questionable methods.

7. Don't encourage customers to break binding contracts with your competitors. This does *not* mean that you shouldn't encourage customers to switch over to you. You should try to convince them to switch brands, but without breaking any binding contracts.

8. Don't spread stories about particular customers to your competitors. Even if a customer is out of favor, don't take it upon yourself to tell your counterparts at competing companies that they shouldn't do business with him. Credit information about customers sometimes may be exchanged, but this should be done through your credit department and cleared by your lawyers.

Seven

DEVELOPING
NEW
PRODUCTS

New product development normally is a joint effort of the technical personnel and the marketing department. Creation of a new product may involve entirely new inventions or simply new varieties of existing items. If the product is truly innovative, it may be patentable, or it may involve trade secrets which need to be protected. A new brand name may have to be created, unless the new product is going to be sold under an existing trademark. In any event, packaging will have to be designed for the new item, and certain labeling may be required, either on the packaging or on the product itself.

The law intrudes upon all of these aspects of new product development, sometimes to provide protection, sometimes to impose obligations. The laws involved are often very specific and complex, and necessitate the advice of specialists. Marketing professionals generally will never even consider bringing new products to market without the advice of a lawyer, but it is still important for them to understand what protection the law provides and what the law demands, so that they will know what to ask for, and what to expect.

BRAND IDENTIFICATION

Once the technical folks have conceived of a new product, either with or without the instigation of the marketing department, the marketing people must decide how to package it. This requires selection of a brand name and a logo. It requires a package design. It also may require compliance with an array of government regulations. No one knows better than marketing executives that packaging often can be as important to the success of a product as what goes inside. The law affords considerable protection to brand names and package design, but it also imposes a galaxy of obligations, particularly with regard to such items as food, drugs and tobacco products, and to clothing.

Creating a Brand.

New lines often require new trademarks, and while marketing executives are not going to undertake the task of securing trademark protection themselves, they should know what safeguards are available. Under the Federal Trademark Act (which is also known as the Lanham Act), a trademark can consist of any words or symbols used to distinguish one supplier's products from those of others. A "service mark" accomplishes the same thing in the case of services.

Trademarks perform important functions which are at the very heart of marketing. They not only distinguish one supplier's products from others, but they may also signify that all the products bearing the trademark are of similar quality. Trademarks provide customers with assurance that they can purchase products of the same brand over and over again, and enjoy the same level of quality for each product every time.

Years ago, the law required trademarks to be used solely to identify products coming from the same manufacturer or other source, much the way the "Perrier" trademark still identifies water originating from a single spring. As the law developed during this century, the use of trademarks as symbols of quality became recognized, even if the trademarked products were obtained from a number of unrelated sources. This permitted trademarks like "Fuller" and, more recently, "Zenith," "Plymouth" and "Chevrolet" to be placed on goods obtained from a number of manufacturers. It also permitted trademark owners to license their trademarks to manufacturers, each of whom would be authorized to make and sell products under the mark, the way trademarks such as "Pierre Cardin" and "Sesame Street" are now licensed.

These changes in the function of trademarks have had profound ramifications on the politics of distribution, because they have permitted wholesalers and retailers to become owners of product trademarks and to control their own brands. Under the original "single source" theory of trademarks, only the manufacturer or other producer could own a trademark. Once that requirement disappeared, it became possible for wholesalers and retailers to own them as well. An example of a trademark owned by a retailer is the well-known "Kenmore" trademark of Sears, Roebuck & Company. Sears selects its suppliers, and decides which products will bear the "Kenmore" name. An example of a trademark owned by a wholesaler is "Cuisinart." For years the food processors sold in this country under the "Cuisinart" trademark were manufactured by a single manufacturer in France, but the trademark was owned by the wholesaler/importer. Eventually, the importer decided to switch to a manufacturer located in Japan. The French manufacturer was left to market its products here under its own trademark, "Robot Coupe," a name which was previously unknown on these shores. The goodwill built up in the "Cuisinart" trademark remained the property of the original importer.

It often happens that whoever owns the trademark will become the "channel leader," imposing terms on those at other levels in the channel of distribution. Traditionally, the manufacturer owned the trademark and could exert influence over the wholesalers and retailers. But where a retailer or wholesaler becomes the owner of the trademark, he often can exercise leadership up the line, particularly where the trademark has strong consumer acceptance. In some situations, the trademark owner is not in the channel of distribution at all. It may be a motion picture company or cartoon publisher as with the "Star Wars" and "Peanuts" marks, which are licensed for a wide variety of merchandise.

Not every would-be brand name can qualify as a trademark. If a name is considered merely "descriptive" of the product, without distinguishing it from the products of other suppliers, it will not be recognized as a trademark. Lawyers refer to this distinguishing function of a trademark's words as their "secondary meaning." To illustrate, the word "Personal" probably would not qualify as a trademark for a personal computer, but more arbitrary and fanciful words, such as the names of fruits, would.

At the other end of the spectrum, some trademarks can be so distinctive that the "dilution doctrine" embodied in state law will prohibit others from using them not only on the same type of goods that the trademark owner is marketing, but on any goods at all. When trademarks are as distinctive as "Kodak," "Rolls-Royce" or "Cartier," the trademark owner's reputation may suffer if these marks are placed on any types of products. In some instances such dilution also could hinder the trademark owner's ability to diversify into other markets.

Trademark Registration.

Normally, trademarks should be registered with the United States Patent and Trademark Office. This affords trademarks the greatest protection, although somewhat more limited protection may be afforded under state and federal law without any registration. Before a trademark is used, a search is conducted to determine whether the same trademark or a confusingly similar trademark already has been registered by someone else for the same or similar products. If the mark checks out, it should be put to use promptly. By law, priority in registering a trademark goes to the first party who uses it, not the first one who thinks of it. This does not require an immediate full-scale rollout of a new product, however. Limited use normally will suffice, but it must involve interstate commerce in order to be eligible for federal registration. This limited use usually can be accomplished simply by making an interstate sale of some quantity of products bearing the new trademark. In the case of services, where no physical product exists, it will suffice simply to advertise the service mark in interstate commerce, so long as the service it represents actually is being performed somewhere.

Once this is done, application may be made to the Patent and Trademark Office for registration. Registration ordinarily will be granted so long as the content of the mark is not immoral or deceptive, the mark is not confusingly similar to another mark already being used on a similar product, and the mark is not "merely descriptive." Registration accomplishes several significant purposes. It tells the world who owns the trademark, permitting subsequent searchers to find it. It allows the Customs Bureau to exclude infringing goods shipped from abroad. It also confers jurisdiction on federal courts to hear infringement suits brought by the trademark owner against similar trademarks and to forbid their use nationwide. Registration will be considered "prima facie" evidence of the trademark's validity in court, meaning that the other party will be obligated to come forward with evidence of invalidity, or else the mark automatically will be considered valid.

Enforcing Trademark Rights.

The right to sue for infringement is one of the most important rights a trademark owner has. The penalties for infringement can be steep: confiscation of the infringing goods, injunction against future infringement, forfeiture of the infringer's profits, reimbursement of the trademark owner's lost profits, trebled in certain cases, and payment of the trademark owner's litigation costs including, in aggravated cases, his attorneys' fees. Under the Trademark Counterfeiting Act of 1984, the owner of a registered trademark may have even greater rights to proceed against knowing counterfeiters, and trademark counterfeiting is now a federal crime, punishable by heavy fines and up to five years in jail.

The owner of a trademark must take certain steps to protect his rights in order to be able to enforce them, however, and some individual within each organization must take responsibility to ensure that this is done. Trademark notices should be included whenever the mark is used, usually by employing the familiar letter "R" within a circle if the mark is registered. In addition, the registration with the Patent and Trademark Office must be kept in effect. The trademark must continue to be used. And, if the trademark is licensed to others, strict quality control must be exercised over the products those people offer for sale under the trademark.

The licensing of trademarks to others who actually manufacture licensed products has raised some fascinating questions. The quality control requirement obligates the licensor to take steps to insure that all products manufactured and distributed by his licensees are of acceptable quality. How much control is enough to satisfy this obligation is not always entirely clear. Most trademark owners are extremely protective of their marks, however, and take the control obligation very seriously. This normally includes sampling and on-site inspections as well as other measures.

Gray Goods.

Another issue which arises with licensing is the territorial separation of the licensees. As we have seen earlier, a supplier normally may impose territorial restrictions on his dealers in this country to keep them from competing against one another, and the same principle generally applies to trademark licensees. Trademark licensing is often international in scope, however, and in this event the situation becomes more complicated.

Internationally, the "freeriding" problem described earlier has manifested itself in the so-called "gray market" or "gray goods." To illustrate, a trademark owner may license an American company to sell his product under his trademark in the United States only. At the same time, he may license other companies to sell the trademarked product in other parts of the world. If the wholesale prices abroad become significantly lower than the prices charged in the United States, importers may begin purchasing the goods overseas at low prices and bringing them in.

This may look like a problem which can be solved simply by restricting the overseas licensees to selling only for resale outside the United States, but matters have become more complicated because United States Customs officials, relying on the customs laws, have sought to prohibit any efforts to block importation of goods which bear genuine trademarks. The Antitrust Division of the Justice Department has taken the contrary position, contending that the owner of the American trademark should be able to keep these "gray goods" out of the country. To say the least, this issue is not yet free of doubt. There are now many examples of companies finding themselves in this quandary, and a good illustration involves the gray goods market which developed several years ago for Mamiya cameras.

CASE HISTORY: Focusing on Gray Goods.

Camera buffs will recognize the name Mamiya as one of Japan's leading manufacturers of photographic equipment designed for professional photographers. Mamiya's practice was to sell its products outside Japan entirely through J. Osawa & Company, which served as its exclusive overseas distributor. Osawa, in turn, did business with a number of distributors throughout the world, but with only one distributor for the United States, then known as Bell & Howell : Mamiya.

Bell & Howell : Mamiya spent millions promoting the Mamiya line in this country. It also offered written warranties to consumers here. Before long, however, it discovered that Masel Supply Company, a Brooklyn, New York wholesaler, had begun importing Mamiya camera equipment and selling it to retailers in the United States at substantially lower prices, without any warranties. Masel was buying the equipment—which turned out to be genuine Mamiya merchandise—from a wholesaler in Hong Kong. That wholesaler, in turn, had been acquiring the goods lawfully from Osawa.

Bell & Howell : Mamiya, however, not only had been designated as Osawa's exclusive distributor for the United States; it also owned the Mamiya trademarks here. When it discovered that it was being undercut by Masel, it curtailed its own advertising outlays and sued Masel for trademark infringement on the ground that Masel was selling goods under the Mamiya trademarks in this country without authorization.

But Masel was selling the genuine article. The Mamiya trademarks were affixed to those goods by the manufacturer in Japan, and the manufacturer owned the trademarks there. Masel resisted, raising several questions:

1. Should Masel have been permitted to sell these products in the United States under the Mamiya trademarks? How was Bell & Howell : Mamiya injured? Was its exclusive distributorship simply worth less because of the manner in which these products were being distributed worldwide? Would it change matters to know that it was owned 93 percent by Osawa and 7 percent by Mamiya?

2. Would it have made a difference if Masel had placed labels on the boxes notifying consumers that the products were being sold without warranties, or that Masel was offering its own warranty?

As noted earlier, there presently is a split within the agencies responsible for enforcement as to whether exclusion of gray goods should be permitted. There is also a split among the courts which have examined these cases. In the Mamiya case, the lower court issued a preliminary injunction halting Masel's sales, but the appellate court vacated the injunction. Eventually, the case was settled. Until the issues are finally resolved, care must be exercised in each case to assure that an international marketing plan will work out as intended, without opening up the possibility of lawsuits. This is the worst of all possible worlds for business decision-makers, and hopefully the issue will soon be resolved.

Generic Terms.

Apart from licensing problems, marketing executives also should be sensitive to the fact that trademarks can be lost entirely if the word or words used for the trademark creep into the language and become "generic." If Otis were to introduce a brand of moving stairs called "Escalator" and everyone started calling them "escalators," the trademark protection of the term could be lost—and this is exactly what happened some years ago. "Linoleum" was once a trademark. So was "thermos," and "cellophane" and "yo-yo." Recent federal legislation specifies that the test for determining whether a registered trademark has become generic will turn on the "primary significance of the registered mark to the relevant public."

But how can you protect against this phenomenon when people you don't know, some of whom don't even buy your product, are carelessly tossing your name about in conversation? The most common safeguard is always to use the generic term alongside the trademark, on packages, advertising and everywhere else. Even if the public loves to refer to your product simply by your name (an enviable position from a marketing standpoint, to be sure), you must always fit in that generic term. This is why we have come to know "Kleenex" facial tissues, "Formica" laminated plastic and "Band-Aid" plastic bandages. Similarly, you should never use your trademark in the possessive case, or in the plural, since this may tend to make the trademark a part of common speech. Another safeguard is the placement of "informational" advertising which unmistakably puts the public on notice that your product's name is a registered trademark. Such ads can be both educational and entertaining. Still another safeguard, of course, is always to use the "R" in a circle next to the mark.

Designing Packaging.

Unless you market fresh fruit, you usually cannot just slap a trademark on your product and deliver it. Products need packaging, and package design is an art in itself. Lawyers commonly use the term "trade dress" to refer to packaging and labeling, including shape, color, design and style of lettering.

If a competitor adopts confusingly similar packaging, he may not be committing actual trademark infringement, but he may be in violation of some broader provisions of the Federal Trademark Act, as well as state law on unfair competition. Packaging can run afoul of the law when the overall impression it makes on the ordinary consumer is likely to create confusion as to the source of the product. A supplier may not copy another supplier's packaging to such an extent that consumers are likely to select the look-alike package by mistake.

One clever method sometimes employed to demonstrate a likelihood of confusion is to pass out "cents-off" coupons for the original product at the entrance to a store, and then monitor which products are purchased by consumers presenting the coupon at the cash register. If an appreciable percentage of consumers bring the copycat product to the check-out counter claiming the cents-off refund, that product's packaging may well be unlawful.

To prevail on a trade dress claim, a plaintiff in most states must first prove that his own packaging has acquired "secondary meaning"—in other words, that the public has come to associate his particular packaging with his brand. If consumers do not associate that particular packaging with the brand to begin with, they arguably cannot be confused by similar packaging. Also, the plaintiff must be able to demonstrate that his package design is not simply functional, since functional improvements in package design will not be protected as trade dress. If these requirements are met, the law will protect distinctive package design, and a supplier need not sit by and permit his competitors to flood the market with look-alike products.

Labeling and Government Regulation.

Not everything that goes into package design is up to the supplier anymore. Increasingly, package configuration and labeling is becoming subject to a sometimes dizzying array of federal, state and even local regulation. From health warning labels to bottle deposit requirements, packaging restrictions have become a way of life.

Marketing executives should make certain that a legal expert has examined any new packaging and checked for compliance with applicable law as soon as an initial package design has been set. Failure to comply can prove very costly, and it is far preferable to get it right the first time.

There is no need to present an exhaustive catalogue of packaging regulations here, and it will suffice to scratch the surface. On the national level, the Federal Trade Commission has general authority to control deceptive labeling. In addition, the Food and Drug Administration has authority over the packaging and labeling of food, drug and cosmetic products, and the Environmental Protection Agency and other agencies impose certain requirements on some products as well. At the state level there often are comparable agencies as well as other specific packaging laws. Even local counties and municipalities sometimes get into the act, often through their consumer affairs bureaus.

There is a federal Fair Packaging and Labeling Act on the books which generally requires "consumer" product labels to identify the type of product being sold, the name and address of the supplier, and, where applicable, the quality of the contents and the size of each serving. The Act also authorizes the FTC and FDA to issue regulations on a product-by-product basis covering such items as ingredient statements, package size characterizations and standards, "slack-fill" packaging, and sales price representations. These regulations can be quite specific. Note, however, that regardless of any ingredient-listing requirements, secret formulas or recipes do not have to be revealed. Also note that if a product does not fall within the definition of a "consumer commodity," the Act will not apply at all.

The Federal Trade Commission enforces this legislation, and its remedial powers are broad. It may prohibit future advertising of an offending product unless certain affirmative disclosures are included. It also may order "corrective advertising," and it may institute civil suits on behalf of consumers to recover monetary damages.

Rolling out a new product presents headaches enough without the nightmare of outlaw packaging. While this is an area to entrust to an expert, it is useful for everyone involved in designing packaging to be cognizant of the basic requirements for their industry before the design work is even begun.

PRODUCT DESIGN

Innovative designs for new products and other new inventions are themselves candidates for protection under either the patent laws or other related areas of the law. If such protection is available, it can have a dramatic effect on the success of a new product. This is not the place for an extensive discussion of the patent laws, but marketing executives should be aware of the fact that product innovations can enjoy considerable protection from competition under the law.

Patents.

Patents exclude others from making or selling a patented article without the consent of the patent owner for a period of seventeen years. (In the case of certain drugs the term may be extended to make up for any time lost as a result of delays in obtaining regulatory approval.) So called "utility" patents are issued for processes, machines and manufactured articles. "Design" patents are issued for ornamental designs incorporated into products. To be patentable, a product, process or design must be novel and cannot be merely an obvious extension of existing "prior art." Patent applications are not easy to prepare, and the advice of an expert in this field is essential.

As with trademarks, the owner of a patent can sue copycats for infringement. Remedies include damages and injunctions against future infringement. Of course, the owner also is entitled to license the patent and collect royalties for its use.

Utility patents can provide important advantages for the marketing of a product, since no other product quite like the patented one will be available from other suppliers for years. The law recognizes that there is an inherent inconsistency between the antitrust laws, which are designed to foster competition, and the patent laws, which are meant to delay competition, but this is what Congress intended. Antitrust intrudes upon the protections of a patent only when the patent owner tries to extend his power beyond the limits fixed by the patent itself. For example, a patent owner may not be allowed to impose a tie-in, requiring his customers to purchase non-patented articles in order to obtain the patented product. Also, if the patent helps to catapult the supplier into the position of a monopolist, certain other consequences may flow from this vaunted position, as discussed in earlier chapters. Generally, however, most innovators find that a patent is well worth having.

Copyrights.

The copyright laws confer protection to original works which can be printed, recorded or "fixed" in any other manner. The law affords the owner of the copyright the sole right to reproduce and distribute the work, display or perform it, and authorize others to do so during the author's lifetime and for fifty years thereafter. Copyrights will not confer protection on new products as such, unless the products by their nature qualify for a copyright. For suppliers of books, records, motion pictures, computer software and even wrapping paper, copyrights naturally are of prime importance. (Computer chips may also be eligible for protection similar to a copyright for a term of ten years under a recently enacted federal law which applies to so-called "mask works.") For other suppliers, copyrights still can become important in connection with protecting their labels and their advertising.

Advertising and promotional material can be copyrighted in most cases, to protect it against plagiarism by competitors. A writing need not be Shakespeare to be eligible for a copyright.

But it must be registered with the United States Copyright Office in order for its owner to secure federal copyright protection and be able to sue for infringement. Copies of the protected work which are released to the public should include a copyright notice consisting of the year of first publication, the name of the copyright owner and the letter "C" in a circle.

Trade Secrets.

One other form of protection for new products comes from the law of trade secrets. Trade secrets can be protected against appropriation by others—whether by means of industrial espionage, hiring away knowledgeable employees or through other means—provided that the firm which possesses the trade secrets takes the necessary steps to safeguard them.

The principal disadvantage of having a trade secret, as compared with a patent, lies in the fact that if the secret is revealed, other than by illegal means, it is lost. If others can take a product apart, for example, and "reverse engineer" a duplicate, any secret embodied in the product's design evaporates. Also, if others learn of the secret through any lapse in secrecy, no matter how brief, the secret is gone forever. On the other hand, the principal advantage of a trade secret over a patent is that potentially it can be preserved indefinitely, while patents pass into the public domain after seventeen years. Also, trade secret protection may extend to some innovations that would not be patentable in any event.

A recognized trade secret can be a formula, a process, a pattern or any other information used in business which affords a competitive advantage. It can be a customer list. It can be the formula for "Coca-Cola" or "Pepsi-Cola," or "Benedictine" or "Chanel No. 5." Whatever it is, it will be afforded trade secret protection only if it is not known outside its holder's business, it is of competitive value, and it has been adequately safeguarded.

To maintain secrecy, the holder of this kind of information should keep anything revealing the secret from open view. Employees having access to the secret information should be re-quired to sign nondisclosure agreements prior to their employment, promising not to reveal the secret either during their term of employment or afterward. An example of such an agreement is presented in **Form 8.** The same type of written promise also may be required of outside vendors who supply elements of a secret combination of ingredients and may have access to all or part of the secret. And naturally, if the secret is recorded in writing, the documentation should be kept in a safe and closely controlled. Where these precautions are followed faithfully, a trade secret can be preserved indefinitely.

Preventing others from duplicating your product can be just as important to a successful marketing program as con-vincing customers to buy it. Whether by patent, copyright or trade secret, having a lock on the product itself can be the key to success. Add a distinctive trademark, package design and ad-vertising which others may not copy, and you have a running start on the competition.

FORM 8
NONDISCLOSURE AGREEMENT

Brutal Noodle Company
100 Prudent Boulevard
Somewhere, U.S.A. 99999

Dear Sirs:

I recognize that is vital to the Brutal Noodle Company ("the Company") that valuable
technical and nontechnical information, not
generally known to the trade or public, be kept
secret and confidential. Accordingly, in consideration of and as a condition to my employment
by the Company (or, if I am now employed by the
Company, the continuation of my employment beyond the date of this letter), it is agreed as
follows:

1. I shall not, either during my employment by
   the Company or thereafter, disclose or otherwise make accessible to anyone in any manner whatsoever (except as authorized by the
   Company in the regular course of my employment), or use in competition with the Company, any secret or confidential information, whether or not patentable, including
   without limitation information relating in
   any way to customers, products, processes
   and services of the Company or of any business
   entity affiliated with the Company, which
   becomes known to me during my employment by
   the Company.

2. Any discovery, process, design, invention or
   improvement which I make or develop during my
   employment by the Company, whether or not
   during my regular working hours or on the Company's premises, and which falls within the
   scope of the Company's business or research

activities as then conducted or contemplated, shall belong to the Company and shall
be promptly and completely disclosed to the
Company. During my employment and thereafter, I shall, without additional compensation, execute and deliver to the Company
any instruments or transfer and take such
other actions as the Company may request to
carry out the provisions of this paragraph,
including the execution of patent applications and other supporting documents. Any
copyrightable material which I create during
my employment by the Company, whether or not
during my regular working hours or on the Company's premises, and which falls within the
scope of the Company's business or research
activities as then conducted or contemplated, similarly shall belong to the Company, and I agree that the Company may claim
authorship as my employer, or list my name as
the author in copyright applications concerning such material, as the Company
chooses.

3. Upon termination of my employment by the Company for any reason, I shall return to the
Company all documents and copies of documents, including without limitation correspondence, memos, drawings or diagrams,
which were prepared or received by me and
which relate in any way to my service with the
Company, unless I first obtain the Company's
written consent to the contrary.

4. Since a breach of the provisions of this letter would injure the Company in a way that
could not adequately be compensated for by
damages, I agree that the Company may, in addition to its other rights, obtain an injunction against any actual or threatened
violation by me, and no bond or other security
shall be required in connection with the injunction.

5. If any provision of this letter is adjudged
   invalid or unenforceable, the remaining
   provisions shall continue in effect.

6. The provisions of this letter shall be governed by and construed in accordance with the
   laws of the State of _____ applicable
   to agreements made and to be performed
   therein.

                    Agreed: _____

_____

Witness

Eight

CONSUMER RELATIONS

Consumer relations has become a fashionable element of marketing lately, as company after company discovers the utility of setting up "800" numbers and replacing the "Complaint Department" with the "Customer Service Bureau" and the "Consumer Hot Line." This was not always true, and several years ago the government stepped in and established a series of consumer protection laws at various levels, regulating such things as warranties, recalls and consumer financing. These laws have become firmly established, and marketing executives should have some basic familiarity with them.

WARRANTIES

At one time, a consumer warranty was virtually anything the seller said it was, and *caveat emptor* was the order of the day. In sales between "merchants," including manufacturers, wholesalers and retailers, the Uniform Commercial Code provided certain warranty requirements and restrictions, which afforded a measure of protection. For the consumer, however, the law presented a hodge-podge, and warranty protection was often illusory.

To bring some order to this chaos, Congress enacted a federal warranty law in 1974 which places certain restrictions on consumer warranties. The law does not actually require suppliers to provide any warranty at all, but when a warranty is provided, it must now comply with certain guidelines. The law applies only to written warranties, not to oral representations. Some oral assurances, however, may be subject to state law.

The federal law applies only to "consumer products," although this term has sometimes been given rather broad definition. The law also is limited to sales made to consumers, and excludes sales to resellers, such as wholesalers and retailers. (Resellers are often afforded rights under the Uniform Commercial Code, however, as noted above.) The category of "consumers" includes any subsequent owners of the product during the life of the warranty, unless the warranty period is specifically limited to the period of original ownership.

If the law applies, a supplier offering a written warranty on a product with a price of more than fifteen dollars must make certain disclosures. These include: (1) any limits on the persons to whom the warranty is extended, unless all consumer-owners during the warranty period are covered; (2) specification of the products, parts or components included in and excluded from the warranty; (3) an explanation of what will be done in the event of a defect, malfunction, or failure to conform to the warranty; (4) the commencement date of the warranty period if it is not the date of purchase; (5) instructions for obtaining performance of any warranty services; and (6) information regarding any informal dispute resolution mechanisms which the supplier may have chosen to adopt.

In addition, if there is any limitation imposed on the duration of "implied" (i.e., unwritten) warranties, this must be accompanied by a statement that some states do not allow such a limitation, so it may not apply. If there is a limitation on "incidental" or "consequential" damages, the same type of statement must be included. Incidental damages are normally indirect costs incurred as a result of product failure, such as the cost of taking a taxi home if your new bicycle breaks down twenty miles away. Consequential damages include costs incurred as a result of a chain of events precipitated by a product failure, such as the cost of replacing your neighbor's garden if your riding mower goes out of control due to a defect and knocks down his fence, allowing rabbits to get in at night.

Finally, any warranty covered by the federal law must include a statement notifying the consumer that while the warranty confers specific rights, the consumer may also have other rights which vary from state to state.

Full or Limited Warranties.

The federal law requires that all warranties for consumer products costing more than ten dollars must be designated as either a "full warranty" or a "limited warranty." (The FTC takes the position that the word "guarantee" may mislead consumers, and the Commission discourages its use.) All warranties which do not meet the criteria for a full warranty are automatically considered limited warranties. On the other hand, all warranties identified with the word "full" will be considered full warranties, even if this was not the intent. For example, if a seller describes a warranty lasting fully five years as a "Full Five Year Warranty," it may be considered a "full" warranty even if the seller intended to offer only a limited warranty for a "full five years."

A supplier who offers a full warranty is obligated to repair any defect or malfunction in the product without charge, or else replace it. If the product can only be used when installed, replacement must include removal and new installation. If the warrantor decides to repair the product, he must be able to repair it successfully within a reasonable number of attempts, or else the consumer may demand replacement or a refund instead. Also, if the supplier determines that neither repair nor replacement is possible or commercially practical, a full refund will be permitted at the supplier's discretion. Full refunds are also permissible in all cases if this is what the consumer prefers and if the supplier agrees.

A full warranty may not contain limitations on the duration of implied warranties, and any limitation of consequential dam-

ages must be prominently displayed. Limited warranties, on
the other hand, may limit the length of any implied warranty to
the life of the written warranty. Also, full warranties may not
be conditioned on the performance of unreasonable duties on
the part of the consumer. For example, it may be unreasonable
to require the consumer to return the product in its original
packaging.

Warranty Registration Cards.

Many suppliers make a practice of utilizing warranty registration cards which record the names of consumers holding
the warranties, and may at the same time provide a very effective device for gathering marketing information from those consumers who already have selected the product. Under the
federal warranty law, the timely return of registration cards may
not be made a condition for extension of a "full" warranty, but
it is a permissible precondition for "limited" warranties, provided that this fact is disclosed in advance, and that the requirement is not merely a ploy to improve the response for survey
purposes.

All types of warranties, however, may at least suggest the
return of a card as one means of showing proof of the date of
purchase. Such a suggestion must be accompanied by disclosure of the fact that failure to return the card will not affect the
consumer's warranty rights so long as the consumer can demonstrate the date of purchase by other means. Warrantors are
also permitted to use voluntary registration systems for certain
purposes such as gathering information regarding the suffi-
ciency of the warranty, product safety or recalls.

Recalls.

Recalls, it should be noted, are not always voluntary. Several government agencies have the power to order recalls or to
require manufacturers to send consumers written warnings re-

garding particular hazards. The Highway Traffic Safety Administration can order recalls whenever it discovers defects relating to motor vehicle safety. The Consumer Product Safety Commission can order recalls of consumer products if its investigations reveal that the products pose substantial hazards. The Food and Drug Administration, the Coast Guard and the Department of Health and Human Services also may order recalls for particular types of products which fall within their jurisdictions. Recalls, of course, may be ordered whether there is a warranty in effect or not.

Tie-Ins.

There sometimes may be a temptation to use a warranty as leverage to "tie-in" the sale of additional products or services. For example, a supplier may try to condition warranty protection on the use of his own accessories, replacement parts or other inputs, or on the use of his own repair facilities at the consumer's expense. The federal warranty law prohibits tie-ins with any warranted product costing more than five dollars unless the tied article or service is provided free of charge. A supplier may not, for example, provide free replacement parts under a limited warranty but require consumers to pay for installation at the supplier's designated service center. A supplier providing both free parts and free labor under a full warranty, however, may require that repairs be performed at specified facilities. Also, the Federal Trade Commission will waive the tie-in prohibition if the Commission is satisfied that the warranted product will only perform properly in conjunction with the tied articles or services.

Warranties have become a common marketing tool, and many consumers have come to expect them. The rules are not difficult, and you should be sufficiently conversant with them to know exactly what it is that you are offering to the public. Otherwise, you may find that your warranty program is even more generous than anyone had intended.

FINANCING

No aspect of retailing has evoked more bad press than financing abuses. Over the years, some highly publicized offenses have given rise to a progression of legislation placing increasingly tight controls on retail financing arrangements. There is no need for most marketing executives to master these laws in any detail, but it is useful to know what the laws cover, and when you might need advice.

Truth in Lending Act.

On the federal level, the Truth in Lending Act requires disclosure of a number of important terms in consumer finance arrangements. It applies to consumer loans up to twenty-five thousand dollars, and to home loans in any amount. It does not apply to loans for the purchase of items primarily used for business, nor does it apply to lenders who do not ordinarily make loans in the ordinary course of their business. Also, it only applies to loans in which a finance charge is imposed, or in which the purchase price is payable in more than four installments (on the theory that the cost of financing in this kind of transaction is really included in the purchase price).

The disclosure requirements of the Truth in Lending Act are detailed and complex. The Federal Reserve Board publishes model disclosure forms, and if a lender chooses to adopt them, he will have some assurance of being in compliance.

The Act also regulates the advertising of credit terms. Financing arrangements may not be advertised unless they are generally available to the public. Also, lenders who use certain "trigger" terms in their advertising may be required to include certain additional information as well. For example, an ad specifying the number of payments of an installment plan must also state the cash price of the product, any down payment which is required, the amount of each payment and the amount of the finance charge expressed as an annual percentage rate. Also, an advertisement for consumer credit which is payable in more than four installments without a finance charge must state that the cost of credit is included in the price.

Fair Credit Reporting Act.

Creditors normally obtain information on the creditworthiness of applicants from numerous sources, including consumer reporting agencies. The Fair Credit Reporting Act regulates the contents and use of the consumer reports generated by such reporting agencies. Individual creditors generally will not be subject to these regulations, provided they do not function as a reporting agency. A creditor is free to request information from other businesses regarding the credit history of a prospective purchaser so long as the information is for the creditor's own use only. The creditor also may pass along information on his transactions with consumers to other businesses or reporting agencies. The creditor must not pass on credit information he receives from others to third parties, however, because this may bring him within the definition of a consumer reporting agency, and expose him to the requirements of the Reporting Act. In any event, the creditor also must be sure that he is in compliance with the federal Equal Credit Opportunity Act, which prohibits discrimination against any credit applicant on the basis of sex, marital status, age, race, color, national origin, religion, receipt of public assistance or good faith assertion of rights under the federal consumer credit laws.

Fair Credit Billing Act.

Complaints about consumer financing arrangements are almost inevitable. Companies which establish credit accounts for consumers are likely to be confronted with disputes over billing charges as a matter of routine. The Fair Credit Billing Act establishes certain uniform procedures for handling complaints about billing errors. It requires creditors to explain and, when appropriate, to correct billing mistakes. To insure that consumers are informed of these procedures, the Act requires creditors to disclose, at the time an account is opened and semiannually thereafter, a statement of consumer rights and obligations under the Act. The Act also requires that periodic billing statements show the address to which billing inquiries may be sent.

Further requirements are imposed when a billing dispute arises. The consumer is required to put billing inquiries in writing, addressed to the specified address, showing the consumer's identity and account number, setting out the amount of the alleged billing error, and stating the reasons for the consumer's belief that an error has been made. The creditor then is obligated either to respond to the consumer inquiry within thirty days, or to acknowledge receipt of the complaint within thirty days and respond within two billing cycles after the complaint has been received. The creditor's response must be either in the form of a correction of the error or a written explanation of why the account statement is correct. If the creditor fails to respond as required, the complaint must be allowed.

Consumer financing, like warranties, is an area requiring expert guidance through the regulatory maze. This is no place for amateurs. If any new warranty or financing arrangement is to be implemented, or any significant changes in your existing programs are contemplated, a careful legal review is a must.

CONCLUSION

If nothing else from this book sticks, two morals should: Don't write needlessly or carelessly. And when in doubt, consult a lawyer.

Letters and memoranda written by marketing executives have spawned many a lawsuit and lost many more. The problem is not with malevolent executives who put their illegal schemes in writing—those people should expect the consequences. The real problem is with executives who put innocent plans in writing but characterize them in ambiguous terms which become open to conflicting interpretations later on. Another problem is with executives who simply describe facts inaccurately. In litigation, each party normally is entitled to inspect relevant documents in the possession of the other side. As a consequence, you must anticipate that your documents will pass into the hands of adversaries some day, and it is critical that sloppy language be avoided in both correspondence and internal memoranda.

Common sense, combined with the most basic understanding of the law, is all that is necessary. Don't write that you want to "crush" your competitor if your intention is only to compete against him vigorously. Don't write that you hope to "dominate" the market within two years if you realistically expect only to be one of several leaders, or if you don't even know what the market is. One recent magazine advertisement boasted unabashedly that the advertised product "dominates its market," when in reality it faces plenty of competition.

Sometimes there is tremendous pressure to write overly optimistic and overly aggressive reports in order to impress a superior, or the shareholders, or the investment community. Often the most explosive (and inaccurate) memos are written by people with the least experience, and more often than not, their plans are never implemented. Yet long after they have moved on, their loose language may achieve great prominence in litigation. This may leave their old boss to testify as best he can that the memo did not mean what it seemed to say, did not present the facts accurately, and never was adopted or even considered seriously by upper management.

The solution to this dilemma is to prevent misleading documents from being written in the first place. This may require writing seminars, scary movies (which are available), or a variety of other measures. In addition, document retention programs, under which documents which are no longer important are routinely discarded after a period of years, can regularly rid the files of outdated paper which nobody clearly remembers or can explain with any accuracy.

Next, we turn to the lawyers. Lawyers are not a cure-all for every problem described in this volume, but knowing when to call on them for legal advice often can save not only time, but embarrassment, vast sums of money, and careers. While this book has pointed out numerous occasions warranting consultation with an attorney, this message must be repeated periodically to be effective, and it must be spread throughout the organization. One way to accomplish this is by distributing a legal handbook, or at least by distributing a legal compliance checklist, to every sales representative and to every marketing executive. One example of this kind of checklist appears on pages 161–163.

A handbook or checklist, of course, is only of value if it is read. To ensure that the message is getting across, it is also important to have an attorney conduct periodic seminars with the "front line" marketing personnel, both to remind them of what the law requires and to sound them out as to what is really going on "in the field"—what the problems are and how to achieve lawful solutions. Helping to identify potential legal problems early, in order to allow for the development of workable solutions, is the essential purpose behind this book. Live interaction between marketing personnel and their attorneys should be an integral part of that process.

In the final analysis, knowing something about the law which applies to marketing can provide tremendous advantages to executives who are engaged in the business of marketing day-to-day. Knowledge of the law will not sell more widgets, but it will allow marketing executives to get on with the job of marketing instead of taking out weeks or months from their careers to review documents, sit for depositions and appear in court. A telephone call for five minutes of legal advice before a decision is finalized can save many boring hours locked away with lawyers, judges and juries later on.

The fact is, virtually every one of the legal conflicts addressed in this book can be avoided if handled with skill and diplomacy. If there are some confrontations that you cannot avoid, at least be sure that you win. If, on the other hand, it turns out that your only exposure to courtrooms comes from the pages of this book, don't be disappointed—you can count yourself the biggest winner of all.

MARKETING LAW COMPLIANCE CHECKLIST

CONSULT COUNSEL *BEFORE*:

1. Before you refuse to sell to a customer or prospective customer.

2. Before you limit customers in their resale of the Company's products, including pricing, territorial operation or customer selection.

3. Before you limit a customer in handling competitive

brands, or require him to take all or a portion of his requirements from the Company.

4. Before you introduce new distribution agreements, or new provisions in those agreements.

5. Before you allocate any scarce products among customers.

6. Before you write or speak with your competitors, or attend meetings with competitors.

7. Before you make significant changes in your prices, price schedules or promotional allowances, including your method of announcing or publicizing these changes.

8. Before you deviate from normal prices or promotional allowances, or offer any customer prices, conditions of sale or services which are more favorable than those being offered to other customers.

9. Before you purchase from any vendor at prices or terms which are more favorable than those you know the vendor is offering to his other customers.

10. Before you respond to any complaint from a supplier, competitor, or customer claiming injury or discrimination.

11. Before you begin marketing a new product, or marketing an existing product in new packaging.

12. Before you introduce a new advertising campaign or selling technique.

13. Before you enter into any acquisition, merger or joint venture.

14. Before you acquire patents or trademarks, or issue patent or trademark licenses.

15. Before you introduce a new warranty, or make changes in existing warranties.

16. Before you join a trade association, submit any information to a trade association or correspond with a trade association (except as to routine matters). Copies of any agenda

or minutes from trade association meetings should be provided to the Legal Department.

17. Before you engage in joint or collective efforts to influence government action by legislative, administrative or executive bodies.

18. Before you respond to requests for information or in-
terviews submitted by any governmental agency.

TABLE
OF
CASES*

Continental T.V., Inc. v. *GTE Sylvania Inc.*, 433 U.S. 36 (1977)

Great Atlantic & Pacific Tea Co. v. *FTC*, 440 U.S. 69 (1979)

Jefferson Parish Hospital District No. 2 v. *Hyde*, 104 S.Ct. 1551 (1984)

Monsanto Co. v. *Spray-Rite Service Corp.*, 104 S.Ct. 1464 (1984)

Simpson v. *Union Oil Co.*, 377 U.S. 13 (1974)

United States v. *Arnold, Schwinn & Co.*, 388 U.S. 365 (1967)

United States v. *Colgate & Co.*, 250 U.S. 300 (1919)

---

*Citations abbreviated "U.S." are to the United States Reports, the official reporter of United States Supreme Court decisions. Citations abbreviated "S.Ct." are to the Supreme Court Reporter, which publishes the texts of Supreme Court opinions earlier than they appear in the United States Reports.

EXCERPTS FROM SELECTED STATUTES

SHERMAN ACT

Section 1

Every contract, combination in the form of trust or otherwise, or conspiracy, in restraint of trade or commerce among the several States, or with foreign nations, is hereby declared to be illegal. Every person who shall make any contract or engage in any combination or conspiracy hereby declared to be illegal shall be deemed guilty of a felony, and, on conviction thereof, shall be punished by fine not exceeding one million dollars if a corporation, or, if any other person, one hundred thousand dollars, or by imprisonment not exceeding three years, or by both said punishments, in the discretion of the court. [15 U.S.C. § 1]

Section 2

Every person who shall monopolize, or attempt to monopolize, or combine or conspire with any other person or persons, to monopolize any part of the trade or commerce among the several States, or with foreign nations, shall be deemed guilty of a felony, and, on conviction thereof, shall be punished by fine not exceeding one million dollars if a corporation, or, if any

167

other person, one hundred thousand dollars, or by imprisonment not exceeding three years, or by both said punishments,
in the discretion of the court. [15 U.S.C. § 2]

ROBINSON-PATMAN ACT

Section 2 [Amending the Clayton Act]

(a) That it shall be unlawful for any person engaged in commerce, in the course of such commerce, either directly or indirectly, to discriminate in price between different purchasers of
commodities of like grade and quality, where either or any of
the purchases involved in such discrimination are in commerce,
where such commodities are sold for use, consumption, or resale within the United States or any Territory thereof or the District of Columbia or any insular possession or other place under
the jurisdiction of the United States, and where the effect of
such discrimination may be substantially to lessen competition
or tend to create a monopoly in any line of commerce, or to injure, destroy, or prevent competition with any person who
either grants or knowingly receives the benefit of such discrimination, or with customers of either of them: *Provided*, That
nothing herein contained shall prevent differentials which
make only due allowance for differences in the cost of manufacture, sale, or delivery resulting from the differing methods or
quantities in which such commodities are to such purchasers
sold or delivered: *Provided, however*, That the Federal Trade
Commission may, after due investigation and hearing to all interested parties, fix and establish quantity limits, and revise the
same as it finds necessary, as to particular commodities or
classes of commodities, where it finds that available purchasers
in greater quantities are so few as to render differentials on account thereof unjustly discriminatory or promotive of monopoly in any line of commerce; and the foregoing shall then not be
construed to permit differentials based on differences in quantities greater than those so fixed and established: *And provided
further*, That nothing herein contained shall prevent persons en-

gaged in selling goods, wares, or merchandise in commerce from selecting their own customers in bona fide transactions and not in restraint of trade: *And provided further,* That nothing herein contained shall prevent price changes from time to time where in response to changing conditions affecting the market for or the marketability of the goods concerned, such as but not limited to actual or imminent deterioration of perishable goods, obsolescence of seasonal goods, distress sales under court process, or sales in good faith in discontinuance of business in the goods concerned. [15 U.S.C. § 13(a)]

(b) Upon proof being made, at any hearing on a complaint under this section, that there has been discrimination in price or services or facilities furnished, the burden of rebutting the prima-facie case thus made by showing justification shall be upon the person charged with a violation of this section, and unless justification shall be affirmatively shown, the Commission is authorized to issue an order terminating the discrimination: *Provided, however,* That nothing herein contained shall prevent a seller rebutting the prima-facie case thus made by showing that his lower price or the furnishing of services or facilities to any purchaser or purchasers was made in good faith to meet an equally low price of a competitor, or the services or facilities furnished by a competitor. [15 U.S.C. § 13(b)]

(c) That it shall be unlawful for any person engaged in commerce, in the course of such commerce, to pay or grant, or to receive or accept, anything of value as a commission, brokerage, or other compensation, or any allowance or discount in lieu thereof, except for services rendered in connection with the sale or purchase of goods, wares, or merchandise, either to the other party to such transaction or to an agent, representative, or other intermediary therein where such intermediary is acting in fact for or in behalf, or is subject to the direct or indirect control, of any party such transaction other than the person by whom such compensation is so granted or paid. [15 U.S.C. § 13(c)]

(d) That it shall be unlawful for any person engaged in commerce to pay or contract for the payment of anything of value to or for the benefit of a customer of such person in the course of such commerce as compensation or in consideration

for any services or facilities furnished by or through such customer in connection with the processing, handling, sale, or offering for sale of any products or commodities manufactured,
sold, or offered for sale by such person, unless such payment
or consideration is available on proportionally equal terms to all
other customers competing in the distribution of such products
or commodities. [15 U.S.C. § 13(d)]

(e) That it shall be unlawful for any person to discriminate
in favor of one purchaser against another purchaser or purchasers of a commodity bought for resale, with or without processing, by contracting to furnish or furnishing, or by
contributing to the furnishing of, any services or facilities con-
nected with the processing, handling, sale, or offering for sale
of such commodity so purchased upon terms not accorded to all
purchasers on proportionally equal terms. [15 U.S.C. § 13(e)]

(f) That it shall be unlawful for any person engaged in commerce, in the course of such commerce, knowingly to induce or
receive a discrimination in price which is prohibited by this section. [15 U.S.C. § 13(f)]

CLAYTON ACT

Section 3

That it shall be unlawful for any person engaged in commerce, in the course of such commerce, to lease or make a sale
or contract for sale of goods, wares, merchandise, machinery,
supplies or other commodities, whether patented or unpa-
tented, for use, consumption or resale within the United States
or any Territory thereof or the District of Columbia or any insular possession or other place under the jurisdiction of the
United States, or fix a price charged therefor, or discount from,
or rebate upon, such price, on the condition, agreement or understanding that the lessee or purchaser thereof shall not use or
deal in the goods, wares, merchandise, machinery, supplies or
other commodities of a competitor or competitors of the lessor
or seller, where the effect of such lease, sale, or contract for sale

or such condition, agreement or understanding may be to substantially lessen competition or tend to create a monopoly in any line of commerce. [15 U.S.C. § 14]

FEDERAL TRADE COMMISSION ACT

Section 5

(a) (1) Unfair methods of competition in or affecting commerce, and unfair or deceptive acts or practices in or affecting commerce, are hereby declared unlawful.

(2) The Commission is hereby empowered and directed to prevent persons, partnerships, or corporations, except banks, savings and loan institutions described in section 18(f)(3), common carriers subject to the Acts to regulate commerce, air carriers and foreign air carriers subject to the Federal Aviation Act of 1958, and persons, partnerships, or corporations insofar as they are subject to the Packers and Stockyards Act, 1921, as amended, except as provided in section 406(b) of said Act, from using unfair methods of competition in or affecting commerce and unfair or deceptive acts or practices in or affecting commerce.

(3) This subsection shall not apply to unfair methods of competition involving commerce with foreign nations (other than import commerce) unless—

(A) such methods of competition have a direct, substantial, and reasonably foreseeable effect—

(i) on commerce which is not commerce with foreign nations, or on import commerce with foreign nations; or

(ii) on export commerce with foreign nations, of a person engaged in such commerce in the United States; and

(B) such effect gives rise to a claim under the provisions of this subsection, other than this paragraph.

If this subsection applies to such methods of competition only because of the operation of subparagraph (A)(ii), this subsection shall apply to such conduct only for injury to export business in the United States. [15 U.S.C. § 45(a)]

LANHAM ACT

Section 43(a)

Any person who shall affix, apply or annex, or use in connection with any goods or services, or any container or containers for goods, a false designation of origin, or any false description or representation, including words or other symbols tending falsely to describe or represent the same, and shall cause such goods or services to enter into commerce, shall be liable to a civil action by any person doing business in the locality falsely indicated as that of origin or in the region in which said locality is situated, or by any person who believes that he is or is likely to be damaged by the use of any such false description or representation. [15 U.S.C. § 1125(a)]

U.S. DEPARTMENT
OF JUSTICE VERTICAL
RESTRAINTS GUIDELINES*

1. PURPOSE OF THE GUIDELINES

These Guidelines explain the enforcement policy of the U.S. Department of Justice ("Department") concerning non-price vertical restraints[1] subject to sections 1 and 2 of the Sherman Act[2] or section 3 of the Clayton Act.[3] They set forth the general principles and specific standards used by the Department in analyzing the likely competitive effects of nonprice ver-

---

*JANUARY 23, 1985

1. These Guidelines deal only with nonprice vertical restraints, which the Supreme Court has ruled are subject to a rule of reason analysis, and with tying arrangements. Resale price maintenance is not treated in these Guidelines. (See discussion of the distinction between price and nonprice restraints at Section 2.4 *infra*.)

2. 15 U.S.C. §§ 1, 2 (1982). Section 1 prohibits "[e]very contract, combination, . . . or conspiracy in restraint of trade." Section 2 prohibits monopolization, attempts to monopolize, and combinations or conspiracies to monopolize any part of trade or commerce.

3. 15 U.S.C. § 14 (1982). Section 3 makes it unlawful to "lease or make a sale or contract for sale of . . . commodities . . . on the condition, agreement or understanding that the lessee or purchaser thereof shall not use or deal in the . . . commodities of a competitor or competitors of the seller or lessor where the effect . . . may be to substantially lessen competition or tend to create a monopoly in any line of commerce."

tical restraints.[4] By stating its policy as simply and clearly as possible, the Department hopes to contribute to the orderly development of vertical restraints case law, and thereby help reduce the uncertainty associated with enforcement of the antitrust laws in this area. A reduction in antitrust uncertainty should assist business planning and encourage the use of lawful vertical practices.

Vertical restraints are arrangements between firms operating at different levels of the manufacturing or distribution chain (for example, between a manufacturer and a wholesaler or a wholesaler and a retailer) that restrict the conditions under which firms may purchase, sell, or resell. Although vertical restraints can take a variety of forms, these Guidelines focus primarily on two major categories of restraints that may give rise to anticompetitive concerns:

> Territorial and Customer Restraints—restrictions on the territory in which, or customers to which, a buyer is permitted to resell goods purchased from the seller, including location clauses, areas of primary responsibility, and profit pass-over arrangements.
>
> Exclusive Dealing Arrangements—requirements that a buyer deal only with a particular seller or that a seller deal only with a particular buyer or group of buyers, including exclusive distributorships, sole outlet provisions, and requirements contracts.

In addition, the Guidelines discuss separately a third category of vertical restraints, tying arrangements, which are requirements that the buyer of a product or service purchase a second, distinct product or service as a condition of purchasing the first.[5]

As the Supreme Court recognized in *Continental T.V., Inc. v. GTE Sylvania, Inc.*, 433 U.S. 36, 54-57 (1977), vertical restraints

---

4. The standards by which the Department analyzes vertical mergers are set forth in U.S. Department of Justice, Merger Guidelines § 4.2.

5. Tying arrangements are discussed in Section 5 of the Guidelines.

may promote competition by allowing a manufacturer to achieve efficiencies in the distribution of its products and by permitting firms to compete through different methods of distribution. In some cases, however, vertical restraints also may be used to facilitate collusion among competitors or to exclude rivals. Therefore, the legality of a vertical restraint in each case depends on its economic effect, assessed under a "rule-of-reason" standard.[6]

The courts have been applying the economic analysis required by *Sylvania* to the facts of particular cases before them, but the method of antitrust analysis in this area remains somewhat uncertain. As a result, businesses may be deterred from using procompetitive vertical practices by the prospect of long and costly litigation with unpredictable results. The economy is harmed when lawful, efficient conduct is avoided because of legal uncertainty. Conversely, the economy is harmed when vertical restraints, on balance, have an anticompetitive effect.

These Guidelines are intended to eliminate as much uncertainty as possible by describing relatively simple standards to analyze vertical restraints. Section 2 discusses the coverage of these Guidelines. Section 3 examines the most prominent procompetitive and anticompetitive effects of vertical restraints. Section 4 outlines the Department's two-step rule of reason analysis. In Step One, the Department uses a market power "screen" to identify cases in which the risk of competitive harm from a restraint is so insignificant that there is no need to inquire further. It should be emphasized that a restraint is not to be deemed somehow suspect merely because it is not screened out under Step One. Failure to be screened out under Step One simply means that more analysis is needed. In Step Two, the Department undertakes a more in-depth analysis, incorporating a variety of other factors, to determine whether a restraint that was not screened out under Step One actually has anticompetitive effects. Section 5 deals with tying arrangements. Section

---

6. For the somewhat different treatment applied to tying arrangements, see Section 5 *infra*.

6 describes market definition principles used by the Department in analyzing vertical restraints.

2. COVERAGE OF THE GUIDELINES

The initial step in analyzing cooperative conduct involving several independent firms is to decide whether the activity falls into a category of conduct that is per se illegal. A restraint found to be in such a category is illegal regardless of its competitive effect.

The per se rule is a special aspect of rule of reason analysis. A restraint is per se unlawful if it has a "pernicious effect on competition and . . . lack[s] any redeeming virtue."[7] For example, naked agreements among competitors to set prices are per se unlawful because they are almost certainly aimed at increasing price and restricting output and they are highly unlikely to offer plausible competitive benefits. More generally, a practice is per se unlawful if it appears highly likely that it will restrict the output of the collaborators or increase their price *and* there is no plausible procompetitive justification for the practice (i.e., there is no plausible argument that the practice actually increases efficiency and consumer welfare).[8]

The Supreme Court has made clear in several recent decisions that the per se rule may not be applied in situations where the conduct in question is reasonably necessary to achieve significant efficiencies or where the requisite "pernicious effect on competition" is absent.[9] The Court's admonition against literal or blind application of per se rules is especially appropriate when dealing with vertical restraints, because experience and

---

7. *Northern Pac. Ry. v. U.S.*, 356 U.S. 1, 5 (1958).

8. *See NCAA v. Board of Regents of University of Oklahoma*, 104 S. Ct. 2948 (1984).

9. *NCAA v. Board of Regents of University of Oklahoma*, 104 S. Ct. 2948 (1984); *Broadcast Music, Inc. v. Columbia Broadcasting System*, 441 U.S. 1 (1979); *Continental T.V., Inc. v. GTE Sylvania, Inc.*, 443 U.S. 36 (1977); and *Northern Pac. R. Co. v. United States*, 356 U.S. 1, 5 (1958).

economic theory suggest that most nonprice vertical restraints do not "always or almost always tend to restrict competition and decrease output."[10]

By providing a relatively simple, easy-to-use analysis that can effectively distinguish truly anticompetitive vertical restraints from all others, these Guidelines should minimize the need to rely on per se rules in this area. These Guidelines should eliminate the need to classify potentially anticompetitive vertical restraints as per se violations of the antitrust laws because of a concern that it is so difficult, time-consuming, and costly to prove an antitrust violation under the alternative—a cumbersome and unfocused rule of reason. Thus, where there are doubts, characterization issues involving vertical restraints should be resolved in favor of a determination that the rule of reason, rather than the per se rule, applies.

2.1 Distinguishing Between Vertical Restraints and Horizontal Restraints

The appropriate focus of the antitrust laws should be the effect of restraints on competition among manufacturers of competing brands—interbrand competition—rather than their effect on competition among dealers of a single manufacturer's brands—intrabrand competition. The competitive consequences of restraints that affect interbrand competition are different from those that only affect intrabrand competition. Restraints on interbrand competition may have a significant negative impact on economic welfare. By contrast, vertical restraints that only affect intrabrand competition generally represent little anticompetitive threat and involve some form of economic integration between different levels of production or distribution that tend to create efficiencies.

Even though, in some cases, intrabrand restraints can be characterized as horizontal agreements because competing

---

10. *Broadcast Music Inc. v. Columbia Broadcasting System*, 441 U.S. 1, 19-20 (1979).

dealers act in concert, it is inappropriate to treat intrabrand agreements in the same manner that other horizontal agreements are treated. Such restraints can have no effect that could not also be obtained through the unilateral action of the manufacturer of the particular brands in question. An intrabrand agreement should not create the inference that a restraint is being "imposed" on a manufacturer. A manufacturer's dealers may be in a far better position than the manufacturer to observe shortcomings in the current method of distribution that reduce the ability of the manufacturer's brands to compete with other brands.[11] If a single manufacturer complies with a requests [sic] of its dealers, the resulting restraint would be properly characterized as a vertical restraint imposed by the manufacturer.

The Department will not treat a restraint as horizontal merely because of communication among sellers of a single manufacturer's product. To establish that there is a horizontal agreement among manufacturers or among sellers of more than one manufacturer's brands, the antitrust analysis typically used to establish a horizontal conspiracy will be applied.[12] If, under normal antitrust principles, a restriction is found to be the result of an agreement among distributors of competing brands affecting competition among those brands or of an agreement among competing manufacturers, the agreement is more properly labeled as horizontal.

Vertical restraints adopted as a result of agreement among firms in interbrand competition are far more likely to harm competition than those adopted unilaterally and therefore merit close scrutiny without regard to the structural criteria of the screens below. The Department also will carefully examine any

---

11. See Monsanto Co. v. Spray-Rite Service Corp., 104 S. Ct. 1464, 1470 (1984). The Court in GTE Sylvania recognized that "[t]here may be occasional problems in differentiating vertical restrictions from horizontal restrictions originating in agreements among the retailers." 433 U.S. 36, 58 n.28. The Court did not regard this difficulty as sufficient justification for a per se rule against vertical nonprice restraints. Id.

12. See, e.g., First Nat'l Bank v. Cities Serv. Co., 391 U.S. 253, 288-90 (1968).

agreements not to purchase from or sell to any particular person or type of person among sellers at the same level of distribution. For example, if several retailers agree among themselves not to carry the products of certain manufacturers, the Department will not apply the Step One screens below. Such agreements may be used to foreclose competitors and may have no efficiency justifications.

2.2 Dual Distribution

Some companies choose total vertical integration into distribution rather than reliance on contracts with independent distributors, and, in such cases, vertical integration may well be more efficient and lead to lower prices to consumers. Among possible savings from such vertical integration are more efficient planning, lower transaction costs, better control over performance, quicker implementation of marketing innovations, and better access to market information. Other companies may choose to integrate partially, making some of their sales directly while making other sales indirectly through independent dealers. Such variety in distribution may enable the companies to realize the efficiencies of vertical integration (for example, in dealing with large customers or special orders), while taking advantage of independent distributors in other circumstances (for example, in dealing with smaller customers or ones in more remote geographic areas). "Dual distribution" refers to suppliers' practice of selling to final consumers both directly and through independent dealers.

Situations involving dual distribution have sometimes erroneously been characterized as horizontal, and subjected to a per se analysis, because the supplier also acts as dealer. However, the fact that a supplier also engages in distribution does not make a restraint "horizontal." Accordingly, vertical restraints involving dual distribution will be analyzed in the same manner as other vertical restraints as outlined in Section 4 of these Guidelines, except that the existence of dual distribution affects the calculation of the market structure screen set forth in Section 4.1.[13]

2.3 Distinguishing Between Price and Nonprice Restraints

For many years resale price maintenance has been held to be illegal per se, and so these Guidelines do not apply to resale price maintenance. All vertical restraints, however, even those that result in substantial procompetitive benefits, may have some effect on price. Therefore, it is important to avoid characterizing a particular restraint as resale price maintenance merely because it may have an effect on price. Before characterizing a practice as a price restraint subject to per se condemnation, there must be an agreement between a supplier and its distributors as to resale prices. Thus, if a supplier adopts a bona fide distribution program embodying nonprice restraints, these Guidelines will apply *unless* there is direct or circumstantial evidence (other than effects on price) establishing an explicit agreement as to the specific prices at which goods or services would be resold.

Further, in accordance with *Eastern Scientific Co. v. Wild Heerbrugg Instruments, Inc.*, 572 F.2d 883 (1st Cir.), *cert. denied*, 439 U.S. 833 (1978), if a supplier adopts a bona fide distribution program embodying both nonprice and price restrictions, the Department will analyze the entire program under the rule of reason if the nonprice restraints are plausibly designed to create efficiencies and if the price restraint is merely ancillary to the nonprice restraints.

2.4 Restrictions in Intellectual Property Licenses

These Guidelines also do not apply to restrictions in licenses of intellectual property (e.g., patent, a copyright, trade

---

13. *See* note 27, *infra*. Thus, vertical integration in itself does not raise an antitrust problem unless there is a violation of section 7 of the Clayton Act. *See* Merger Guidelines § 4.2.

secret, and know-how). Such restrictions often are essential to ensure that new technology realizes its maximum legitimate return and benefits consumers as quickly and efficiently as possible. Moreover, intellectual property licenses often involve the coordination of complementary, not competing, inputs. Thus, a rule of reason analysis is appropriate. Unless restrictions in intellectual property licenses involve naked restraints of trade unrelated to development of the intellectual property, or are used to coordinate a cartel among the owners of competing intellectual properties, or suppress the creation or development of competing intellectual properties, the restrictions should not be condemned. However, because the anticompetitive risks and the procompetitive benefits of restrictions in licenses are somewhat different from the potential of typical vertical restraints, the rule of reason analysis may also differ from (and be even more lenient than) that set out in these Guidelines.

2.5 Vertical Restraints that are Always Legal

Certain types of vertical restraints are widely recognized as legal, and are subject to very little antitrust uncertainty. For example, manufacturers may lawfully choose to deal through a limited number of outlets—so-called "selective distribution"—and their mere refusal to sell through other outlets is clearly proper.[14] Moreover, arrangements under which a manufacturer assigns areas of "primary responsibility" to a dealer without imposing absolute territorial limits generally have been upheld by the courts.[15] Likewise, "location clauses," establishing or restricting the outlets from which dealers can sell, have been consistently upheld.[16] Finally, "profit passover" arrangements,

---

14. *Monsanto Co. v. Spray-Rite Service Corp.*, 104 S. Ct. 1464 (1984).

15. *See, e.g., Kestenbaum v. Falstaff Brewing Corp.*, 575 F.2d 564, 572-73 (5th Cir. 1978), *cert. denied*, 440 U.S. 909 (1979); *Santa Clara Valley Distrib. Co. v. Pabst Brewing Co.*, 556 F.2d 942 (9th Cir. 1977); and other cases cited at ABA Antitrust Section, *Antitrust Law Developments* 73-74 n.495 (2d ed. 1984).

16. *See, e.g., GTE Sylvania, Inc. v. Continental T.V., Inc.*, 537 F.2d 980 (9th Circ. 1976) (en banc), *aff'd*, 433 U.S. 36 (1977), *on remand*, 461 F. Supp. 1046 (N.D. Cal. 1978), *aff'd*, 684 F.2d 1132 (9th Cir. 1982) (summary judgment for

whereby a dealer is required to compensate other dealers for sales made in their territories, have been approved, especially where such arrangements are reasonably related to reimbursing dealers for their advertising, promotional, and post-sale servicing efforts.[17] Because these forms of vertical restraints pose negligible anticompetitive risks and have significant potential to enhance efficiency, these Guidelines are not intended to cast doubt on the legality of these forms of vertical restraints and do not apply to them. The Guidelines are directed instead at those airtight vertical restraints (territorial and customer restraints and exclusive dealing arrangements) the legal status of which remains somewhat uncertain.[18]

3. PROCOMPETITIVE AND ANTICOMPETITIVE EFFECTS OF VERTICAL RESTRAINTS

Vertical restraints exist in a variety of forms and combinations and may produce a variety of competitive effects. This section of the Guidelines examines some of the more prominent procompetitive and anticompetitive effects of vertical restraints.

---

defendant); *Golden Gate Acceptance Corp. v. General Motors Corp.*, 597 F.2d 676 (9th Cir. 1979) (summary judgment for defendant); and other cases cited at *Antitrust Law Developments, supra* note 16, at 73 n.491.

17. *See United States v. Arnold, Schwinn & Co.*, 291 F. Supp. 564 (N.D. Ill. 1968), *vacated*, 442 F. Supp. 1366 (N.D. Ill. 1977) (profit passover permitted in final judgment). *Compare Superior Bedding Co. v. Serta Assoc., Inc.*, 353 F. Supp. 1143, 1150-51 (N.D. Ill. 1972) (seven percent passover fee based on gross sales paid to licensees in whose territory sales were made to compensate for advertising and sales expense by that licensee upheld) *with Eiberger v. Sony Corp. of Am.*, 622 F.2d 1068, 1076-81 (2d Cir. 1980) (warranty fee passover unreasonable when it was designed to penalize extraterritorial sales and impede intrabrand competition without enhancing interbrand competition).

18. Airtight territorial and customer restraints impose restrictions on the territory in which, or the customers to whom, a buyer is permitted to resell goods. Similarly, airtight exclusive dealing arrangements explicitly limit the sellers with whom a buyer may deal, or the buyers to whom a seller may sell.

3.1 Procompetitive Effects of Vertical Restraints

In recent years, there has been increased recognition of the procompetitive functions performed by vertical restraints. The following discussion highlights those functions that generally are regarded as the most significant. It is not intended, however, to be an exhaustive list of efficiency-enhancing functions that vertical practices may serve or that should be considered in evaluating the competitive effect of a particular restraint.[19]

First, and perhaps most important, vertical restraints that limit the number of outlets may lower distribution costs by enabling each distributor to obtain scale economies, to spread such fixed costs as facilities and training of service personnel over a higher volume of sales, and thus to lower the cost of distributing a product. Second, restraints such as exclusive distribution may facilitate entry of a new producer into a market by enabling distributors to recover initial market development costs. Third, limiting the number of distribution outlets may be the most efficient method of insuring the provision of pre-sale demonstration and other informational services that consumers want and that are necessary to effective marketing of a technically complex product. In those circumstances, in the absence of vertical restraints a dealer may invest too little in such services because other dealers that do not provide the services may "free ride" on the services that the dealer has provided. By reducing the threat of free-riding, vertical restraints may enable a dealer to capture a significant fraction of the increase in total demand that is generated by his investment in informational services and, therefore, encourage dealers to expend the effort required to provide those services. Fourth, vertical restraints, such as exclusive dealerships, may allow a supplier to protect its invest-

---

19. The reason that a particular restraint is successful in increasing consumer welfare may not be clear until long after the restraint is first used. For that reason, the antitrust laws should not deter business from experimenting with vertical practices that do not pose a substantial anticompetitive risk simply because the practices' procompetitive benefits are unclear.

ment in services provided to dealers (e.g., advertising) by preventing dealers from using those services to sell the goods of other suppliers. Fifth, vertical restraints—for example, requirements contracts—may permit firms to allocate costs or risks among themselves in a manner that may permit the accomplishment of transactions that otherwise would be impossible or at least much less feasible. Finally, vertical restraints can improve product quality and safety and reduce transactions costs in numerous circumstances.

3.2 Anticompetitive Effects of Vertical Restraints

Although vertical restraints generally have a procompetitive or competitively neutral effect, in some cases they may facilitate collusion among competitors or may be used by one or more competitors to exclude their rivals. This Section describes the minimal market structure conditions that must exist before it is plausible that vertical restraints have such anticompetitive effects.

3.21 Facilitating Collusion

Vertical restraints may be used to facilitate collusion among dealers of different suppliers.

For example, dealers may induce all or almost all suppliers of a product to award exclusive territories. This could facilitate collusion among dealers by limiting the number of dealers that must agree to fix prices or restrict output and by protecting colluding dealers within a geographic market from the threat of outside competition in response to supracompetitive prices. In addition, suppliers could police the cartel by replacing uncooperative dealers.

In addition, suppliers may be able to use vertical restraints to facilitate a collusive scheme of their own. In particular, suppliers may attempt to facilitate collusion among dealers where (i) direct collusion among suppliers is impractical or more costly than collusion among dealers, and (ii) suppliers can share in the dealers' supracompetitive profits. Unless both of these conditions are met, it would not be in the economic interest of a supplier to foster the development of market power among its dealers.

Vertical restraints are likely to facilitate collusion only if (after the imposition of the restraints) relatively few dealers account for most sales of the product in the geographic area, relatively few suppliers account for most of the sales in the geographic area, and the practice is widely used by large suppliers in the geographic area. Facilitation of collusion through the use of vertical restraints is unlikely unless the level of the market that instigates the restraints (the "primary market") is relatively highly concentrated (prior to the imposition of the restraints). If the primary market is unconcentrated, the coordination and policing of the competitors' conduct will be very costly, if not impossible, in the absence of an explicit agreement among the competitors.[20] In addition, if the combined market share of the firms in the other market (the "secondary market") is small, the practice is unlikely to facilitate collusion because it is unlikely significantly to increase the effective level of market concentration in the secondary market. Finally, vertical restraints are unlikely to facilitate successful collusion unless entry into the primary market is difficult. If entry is easy, new competitors would quickly enter and undercut attempted collusion.

Thus, vertical restraints are unlikely to facilitate collusion unless three market conditions are met:

(1) Concentration is high in the primary market;

(2) The firms in the secondary market using the restraint account for a large portion of sales in that market; and

(3) Entry into the primary market is difficult.

---

20. If the Department has evidence of such an agreement, it will scrutinize the agreement under normal antitrust principles discussed in Section 2 and will not apply the Step One market structure screen discussed in Section 4.

3.22 Excluding Rivals

It is also possible that vertical restraints—particularly, exclusive dealing—may have the effect of excluding rivals by prohibitively raising either their cost of a vital input or their cost of distribution. For example, in the case of exclusive dealing, a supplier (or group of suppliers acting independently) may require that its dealers not deal in the goods of competing suppliers. This would force rival suppliers either to secure alternative independent dealer outlets or to integrate vertically into distribution. If these two alternatives are much more costly than dealing with the "foreclosed" dealers would have been,[21] rivals of the supplier may be prevented from entering the market or from expanding output, or may be forced to exit the market.[22]

Alternatively, a firm (or firms) at any stage of the manufacturing or distribution chain may enter into long-term exclusive contracts for the supply of a vital input, leaving little or no present production of the input for new entrants or fringe firms. In the short run, a rival firm would be unable to obtain a sufficient amount of the input to allow it to operate at minimum efficient scale, or would be required to use more costly substitutes. Over the long run, a rival firm either would have to enter into the production of the input itself, operate at a suboptimal scale or use more costly inputs until the exclusive contracts with existing firms expire, or rely on new entry into production of the input by others. If these three alternatives are significantly more costly than dealing with the "foreclosed" suppliers would have been, rival firms may be prevented from

---

21. These Guidelines are not intended to penalize firms that develop very efficient distribution systems that make distribution less costly because of, for example, superior management.

22. While vertical restraints may only delay entry, and not block it entirely, the delay may be significant enough to warrant antitrust action. The relevant question is whether entry is delayed for a period that is sufficiently long to affect consumer welfare significantly.

entering the market or from expanding output, or may be forced to exit the market.

An exclusive dealing arrangement is unlikely to be used to exclude rivals unless it has two characteristics: (a) it must significantly raise rivals' costs of gaining access to an input or to distribution facilities, and (b) if the restraint raises a firm's own costs, the firm (or firms) employing this restraint must be able to collect a sufficiently large return from the practice to offset the increase in its (or their) costs caused by the restraint.

In turn, for exclusive dealing to facilitate anticompetitive exclusion, the following market conditions normally must be met:

(1) The "nonforeclosed market" is concentrated and leading firms in the market use the restraint;

(2) The firms subject to the restraint control a large share of the "foreclosed market"; and

(3) Entry into the "foreclosed market" is difficult.

Anticompetitive exclusion is not likely to result from exclusive dealing arrangements if any of these conditions is absent. If the firms in the "nonforeclosed market" using the restraint are small and numerous, they cannot, on an individual basis, foreclose a great deal of the market, or raise their rivals' costs by more than their own (condition one). Furthermore, foreclosing inputs or distribution facilities would present no problem to a firm seeking to expand in or enter into the output market if it could easily enter into the "foreclosed market" itself or count on entry by other firms in response to the increased demand for input production or distribution facilities (condition three). If the restraint does not affect all or a large share of the "foreclosed market," firms can use remaining available capacity (condition two). For example, rivals are unlikely to be foreclosed if a firm signs all of its dealers to exclusive dealing contracts, but its dealers represent only a small proportion of the dealers in the geographic market.

3.3 Vertical Restraints and Regulated Industries

Industries that have entry or rates regulated (such as energy, communications, and transportation) may be subject to competitive distortions that alter the normal economic effects of various business practices, including vertical restraints. Accordingly, the Department may be required to apply a somewhat different analysis to vertical restraints in industries that have entry or rates regulated.

4. COMPETITIVE ANALYSIS OF VERTICAL RESTRAINTS

The Department employs a two-step process to analyze vertical restraints. First, it takes a "quick look" in order to screen out particular restrictions that are extremely unlikely to have any anticompetitive consequences. It does this by roughly defining markets[23] and then applying a simple "market structure screen" against which firms using restraints are evaluated. Uses of vertical restraints that pass muster under this screen, because the firms using the restraints have small market shares, because the restraints are not widely used, or because the restraints are used in markets too unconcentrated for the exercise of market power, are not subjected to further scrutiny. Step One's reliance on easy-to-apply market definitions and rules of thumb is de-

---

23. Market definition is discussed *infra* in Section 6. The Department employs this market definition framework at both stages of its two-step process for analyzing restraints. Under the first step, the Department roughly applies the framework and assesses the class of products subject to a restraint and the geographic area in which firms using a restraint face significant competition. If a restraint is not "screened out" under Step One, the Department will delineate the market more carefully and painstakingly before subjecting the restraint to further scrutiny under Step Two. If the boundaries of the market are immediately apparent—as may often be the case—little or no market definition "fine tuning" may be needed prior to the second step of the analysis.

signed to encourage its use by the courts and by private parties and thereby to facilitate the use of restraints that clearly pose no threat to competition.

Uses of vertical restraints that are not "screened out" in Step One are examined more closely by the Department. (Because even those vertical restraints not "screened out" in Step One are unlikely to have anticompetitive effects, a restraint is not deemed suspect merely because it is not screened out under Step One.) In Step Two, the Department will more carefully delineate the markets in which the restraints operate and then will assess ease of entry, concentration levels, and other factors bearing on the likelihood that market power can be exercised. This "structured rule of reason" identifies those restraints that are likely to have anticompetitive consequences.

4.1 Step One: Market Structure Screen

After having defined product and geographic markets, the Department will employ a "market structure screen" in order to eliminate from further consideration those restraints that, in all likelihood, have no anticompetitive effects. Uses of vertical restraints by firms with small market shares, those restraints operating in unconcentrated markets, and of those that do not cover a substantial percentage of the sales or capacity in the secondary (foreclosed) market, are unlikely effectively to facilitate collusion or to foreclose competitors from the market. Accordingly, if a firm has a very low market share or operates in a market that is unconcentrated or that is not covered extensively by the restraint, it normally cannot use vertical restraints to accomplish an anticompetitive effect, and its use of such restraints will not be challenged.[24]

The Department will employ the following screen in evaluating territorial and customer restrictions and exclusive deal-

---

24. It should be emphasized, however, that horizontal agreements among competitors are not legalized because the firms involved are small or the markets they operate in are unconcentrated.

ing arrangements. The use of a vertical restraint by a particular firm will not be challenged if:

(1) the firm employing the restraint has a share of the relevant market of 10 percent or less; or

(2) the VRI[25] is under 1,200 and the coverage ratio[26] is below 60 percent in the same (e.g., supplier or dealer) relevant market; or

(3) the VRI is under 1,200 in both relevant markets; or

(4) the coverage ratio is below 60 percent in both relevant markets.

------

25. The Vertical Restraints Index (VRI) is calculated by squaring the market share of each firm in the market that is a party to a contract or other arrangement that contains the vertical restraint and then summing the values obtained for firms at the same level of operations. For example, if only two firms in a dealer market employ a restraint, one with a 5 percent and one with a 20 percent market share, the dealer market VRI equals $5^2 + 20^2 = 25 + 400 = 425$. If four suppliers, each with a 25 percent market share employ a restraint, the supplier market VRI equals $25^2 + 25^2 + 25^2 + 25^2 = 625 + 625 + 625 + 625 = 2,500$. If all firms in the relevant market use the restraint, the VRI is equal to the HHI used in merger analysis. (*See* Merger Guidelines § 3.) The maximum possible value of the VRI is 10,000, achieved when there is only one firm in a market and that firm employs a vertical restraint. The VRI reflects both the distribution of the market shares of firms using a vertical restraint and the extent to which it is used in the relevant market.

26. The coverage ratio is the percent of each market involved in a restraint. For example, if 10 suppliers with 5 percent market shares each employ a restraint, the coverage ratio equals 50 percent. The coverage ratio also would equal 50 percent if two 25 percent suppliers (or one 50 percent supplier) used a restraint. In computing the coverage ratio, several problems present themselves. In computing the coverage ratio for the upstream market (e.g., manufacturing if the two markets under consideration are manufacturing and retailing), it frequently is necessary to use shares that are different from those that would be used in merger analysis. The upstream market (e.g., national manufacturing) frequently will have a much greater geographic scope than the downstream market (e.g., local retailing). In such situations, the appropriate market shares for use in computing the coverage ratio in the upstream market are those for sales to firms in the relevant retailing market. Such shares would be used in merger analysis only if price discrimination against that locality were possible. *See* Merger Guidelines § 2.33.

In short, this screen provides four alternative tests that can be applied by a firm considering using a restraint. If any one of the tests is satisfied, the Department will not challenge the use of the restraint in question.[27]

The first part of the screen provides a safe harbor for the use of vertical restraints by any firm having ten percent or less of the market at its level of distribution. Firms with such small shares do not possess market power individually, and are unlikely to be prominent in any cartel, in any agreement to facilitate a cartel, or in any exclusionary scheme. Usually, a cartel or exclusionary scheme requires that firms having far larger mar-

---

In computing the coverage ratio for the downstream market, it is appropriate to make important distinctions according to whether the potential competitive problem is collusion or exclusion. If collusion is the potential problem, the issue is whether the restraints affect a significant proportion of actual sales. Thus, the relevant market should be delineated and market shares should be calculated under the assumption that the restraint is in place, and shares should be measured on the basis of sales or shipments. If exclusion is the potential problem, the extent to which capacity is foreclosed is the issue. Thus, markets should be delineated and shares should be calculated under the assumption that the restraint is *not* in place, and, ideally, shares should be measured on the basis of capacity. Unfortunately, at this stage of the analysis, it generally is not possible to determine whether collusion or exclusion is the potential competitive problem. Therefore, the Department will adopt in Step One whatever approach to market delineation and share measurement produces the largest coverage ratio. In Step Two, a more refined analysis will be conducted if necessary.

Measuring shares in retailing on the basis of capacity may be extremely difficult, particularly with the information likely to be available at early stages of an investigation. As a proxy, the Department may use the number of retailing outlets owned or controlled by a firm in the relevant geographic area as the basis for computing its market share.

27. The screen is applied separately for each vertical practice. There often will be a range of similar practices that are likely to have similar effects on facilitating collusion or exclusion. Very similar practices will be considered the same practice for purposes of applying the screen. Vertically integrated firms will be included in the relevant markets for purposes of doing the required calculations and assumed to be using the practice in question. Partially integrated firms will be assumed to be using the practice in question to the extent that they transfer products internally rather than buying or selling in the market.

ket shares employ restraints, and they, rather than small firms, merit the closest scrutiny. Of course, if there is evidence that a small firm employing restraints is part of an illegal cartel among direct competitors, the Department will not hesitate to investigate its activities.

The second, third, and fourth tests identify situations in which neither collusion nor anticompetitive exclusion is plausible. As previously explained, it is highly unlikely that vertical restraints will be used to facilitate collusion unless the primary market is concentrated and the practice is widely used by leading firms. Moreover, for a vertical restraint to facilitate collusion, the practice must be applied to firms accounting for a large percentage of the secondary market. Furthermore, it is unlikely that vertical restraints will be used to exclude rivals unless leading firms in one market are parties to exclusive dealing and these firms control a large share of the second, "foreclosed" market.

The second test deems vertical restraints legal if either market fails to satisfy the conditions for the primary (nonforeclosed) or secondary (foreclosed) market that are necessary for an anticompetitive effect. For an anticompetitive effect to be plausible, the primary (nonforeclosed) market would have to be at least moderately concentrated and firms employing the restraint would have to account for a large share of the market (i.e., the VRI would have to exceed 1200).[28] For an anticompetitive effect to be plausible, a substantial portion of the secondary (foreclosed) market also would have to be subject to the restraint (i.e., the coverage ratio would have to exceed 60). The third test treats the use of restraints as legal if both markets are unconcentrated or the restraint is not used by the leading firms (i.e., if both markets have a VRI below 1,200) because neither

---

28. A VRI of 1,200 is equivalent to the use of a vertical restraint by one firm with a 34.6 percent market share, by two firms with 24.5 percent market shares each, by three firms with 20 percent market shares each, or by seven firms with 13 percent market shares each. Accordingly, the use of vertical restraints by several relatively large firms—or by one dominant firm—is associated with a VRI or *over* 1,200.

market could be a primary (nonforeclosed) market in which an anticompetitive effect is plausible under these circumstances. The fourth test provides that restraints will not be further scrutinized if substantial portions of both markets are not subject to restraint. Under such market conditions, neither market satisfies the condition in the secondary (foreclosed) market necessary for a restraint plausibly to have an anticompetitive effect.

The Step One screen allows firms to employ the information that is most accessible to them in determining how the Department will assess their restraints. This should encourage the use of procompetitive restraints by making it as simple as possible to decide whether a restraint will be subject to close Departmental scrutiny. Small firms can rely on the first test, and need not concern themselves with market structure. Firms that only have information on one market can use the second test. Firms that have information either on market concentration or on the share of the market under restraint—but not both—can apply the third or fourth test.

Four examples illustrate how the Department's screen will be applied.

Example One. Two suppliers with 8 percent market shares and two dealers with 9 percent market shares employ vertical restraints. Applying the first test, the Department will not challenge the use of vertical restraints by these firms.

Example Two. Two suppliers with 20 percent market shares and one supplier with a 10 percent market share employ territorial and customer restrictions. The supplier market $VRI = 20^2 + 20^2 + 10^2 = 400 + 400 + 100 = 900$. Fifty percent of the supplier market is subject to restraint. Applying the second test, the Department will not challenge these vertical restraints.

Example Three. Five suppliers with 15 percent market shares and three dealers with 19 percent market shares are subject to territorial and customer restrictions. The dealer level $VRI = 19^2 + 19^2 + 19^2 = 361 + 361 + 361 = 1,083$. The supplier level $VRI = 15^2 + 15^2 + 15^2 + 15^2 + 15^2 = 225 + 225 + 225 + 225 + 225 = 1,125$. Applying the third test, the Department will not further scrutinize these restraints.

Example Four. Fifty percent of the supplier market and 55 percent of the capacity in the dealer market are subject to exclusive dealing restrictions. Applying the fourth test, the Department will not further scrutinize these restraints.

The Department recognizes that a national manufacturer (or national distributor) operating in a large number of local markets may be concerned about whether it satisfies the Step One screen in each individual market. It should be emphasized that the Department will *not* further scrutinize a firm's entire network of restraints merely because a restraint fails to pass the Step One screen in a small number of markets. Rather, the Department will only further examine the use of restraints in those markets where the Step One screen is not satisfied. Furthermore, the Department will view the fact that a firm's restraints pass muster under Step One in most markets as tending to indicate that the restraints in those few markets analyzed in Step Two are more likely to be procompetitive than anticompetitive.

4.2 Step Two: A Structured Rule of Reason Analysis

The Department will apply a "structured rule of reason" analysis to those vertical restraints that are not eliminated from consideration under the Step One screen delineated above. The Step One screen merely determines whether two of the minimal conditions that must exist in order for vertical restraints to be anticompetitive are present. Although those conditions are necessary, they are by no means sufficient; in fact, their presence does not even imply that an anticompetitive effect is reasonably likely. Vertical restraints rarely have a significant anticompetitive effect. In Step Two of the analysis, various other conditions are examined to determine whether an anticompetitive effect is likely to be present. In most cases, restraints not "screened out" in Step One will be found not to have an anticompetitive effect through direct evidence of market performance or other evidence indicating that the markets in which the restraint appear are functioning competitively. In addition, other facts may indicate that, under the circumstances, the restraint will not produce a significant exclusionary or collusion facilitating effect. In some cases, further investigation will uncover persuasive evidence indicating that the restraint actually serves an efficient, procompetitive purpose.

The Step Two structured rule-of-reason analysis is not a broad-ranging inquiry into all aspects of the business and industry under examination. Rather, it focuses exclusively on effects on competition. A Step Two structured rule-of-reason analysis proceeds as follows. Having failed under Step One to exclude the possibility that a vertical restraint might promote collusion or the exclusion of rivals, the Department seeks to determine whether the restraint on balance is anticompetitive.[29] After more carefully defining markets, the Department first examines entry conditions at both the supplier and dealer level.

Both collusion and exclusion require that entry be difficult in at least one market. Thus, if entry is easy in both markets, the Department will conclude that the use of vertical restraints is lawful. If entry is easy in just one market, the Department generally will look at other factors to determine the likelihood that an anticompetitive consequence will flow from the vertical restraint under consideration. The finding of easy entry in just one market will cause the Department to conclude that the vertical restraint is lawful if: (1) it is clear that exclusion is the only possible anticompetitive effect of the restraint, and entry is very easy in the foreclosed market; or (2) it is clear that collusion is the only possible anticompetitive effect of the restraint and entry is easy in the primary market.

If entry considerations do not indicate that it is highly implausible that anticompetitive consequences will flow from a restraint, the Department will analyze other factors bearing on the likelihood that the restraint is anticompetitive rather than procompetitive. If, on balance, these other factors suggest that anticompetitive consequences are implausible, the Department will not challenge the restraint.

---

29. The Department recognizes that a vertical practice can have more than one consequence, and that a single practice can have both positive and negative effects on consumer welfare.

4.21 Ease of Entry

In examining a restraint under Step Two, the Department first examines entry conditions at both the supplier and dealer levels. The analysis of entry conditions parallels that used in merger analysis, i.e., the Department will ask whether significant entry would be likely to occur within a relatively short time in the event of a significant and nontransitory increase in price.[30] While there is no single yardstick used to measure ease of entry, several factors may be examined in evaluating relative ease of entry. Entry is relatively difficult if it requires a costly investment in specialized production or distribution facilities or if it can only be accomplished over a long period of time. For example, if entry into the manufacture of a product requires the construction of a high-cost plant that cannot readily be adapted to other uses, entry at the supplier (manufacturing) level is difficult. Entry into a market at the dealer level will be relatively difficult if, for the product in question, it normally takes years for a dealer to establish sufficient goodwill to achieve a significant level of sales. Entry at either the supplier or dealer level may be relatively difficult if commercial success can be achieved only with extensive investments over time in marketing, training, and promotional activities or with operation at a large scale.

Finally, it should be noted that the ease of entry in distribution is assessed with respect to the product under consideration. Thus, for a product sold through supermarkets, the issue is the ease of entering the distribution of that one product—not necessarily the ease of entering grocery retailing. If, however, it were necessary to construct a chain of retailers in order to enter the distribution of a single product, then entry into the distribution of the product could be difficult in the sense that a very large price increase for the product would be necessary to induce entry.

---

30. *See* Merger Guidelines § 3.3.

4.22 Other Factors

If an anticompetitive explanation for the vertical restraint under study cannot be ruled out after an analysis of structural considerations under Step One and of entry conditions, the Department will look at other factors, as explained below.

Where vertical restraints have been in existence for a sufficient length of time to make it possible to evaluate their actual competitive effects, the Department will look primarily to an analysis of those effects in deciding whether or not to challenge the restraints. The Department recognizes that in many instances it may not be possible to determine what actual economic effect vertical restraints may have had. The restraints may have been in effect for too short a time to permit a meaningful analysis of their actual competitive consequences, or for some other reason the results of such an inquiry may be inconclusive. In such instances, the Department will look to the relevant factors that indicate the likelihood that the restraint is anticompetitive. Below is an illustrative list of such factors.

4.221 How high is the VRI and coverage ratio?

In Step Two the Department uses a somewhat more refined delineation of the relevant markets. It also determines whether collusion or exclusion is the more likely competitive problem and which of the two markets is the primary or nonforeclosed market. Having done this, the Department computes the VRI for the primary (nonforeclosed) market and the coverage ratio for the secondary (foreclosed) market. If the recomputed VRI for the primary (nonforeclosed) market falls below 1200 or the recomputed coverage ratio for the secondary (foreclosed) market falls below 60, the Department will deem the restraint lawful. If such is not the case, the Department will take the magnitudes of the VRI and coverage ratio into account in assessing the likely effect of the restraint. The higher the VRI or the coverage ratio, the greater is the likelihood of a significant anticompetitive effect.[31]

4.222 Are conditions in the relevant markets conducive to collusion?

Vertical restraints are more likely to be used to facilitate collusion in markets with conditions conducive to collusion. For example, collusion is a more likely explanation if only the price need be agreed upon (as in the case of homogeneous goods) than if several aspects of a product—such as price, style, and quality—need be coordinated (as in the case of a heterogeneous product). Collusion also is a more likely explanation if there is a history of collusion in the supplier or dealer markets in which the restraints exist than if there is no such history. (For other conditions conducive to collusion, see Merger Guidelines §§ 3.42–3.44.)

4.223 How exclusionary is the restraint?

Whether and to what extent vertical restraints have an exclusionary effect depends on the extent to which they make it difficult for a small or entering firm to secure the inputs needed to operate at efficient scale. If within a reasonably short time a small or entering firm is able to contract for the inputs and distribution outlets needed to operate at an efficient scale on terms equivalent to those achieved by existing firms, then there is no exclusionary effect. A number of factors determine whether such will be the case. In general, the longer the term of a vertical restraint (especially if such a term cannot be justified by the need to encourage investment) the more likely it is that the restraint is exclusionary. For example, large suppliers' exclusive

---

31. As noted above, however, a high VRI and coverage ratio are not sufficient alone to cause the Department to challenge a restraint.

dealing arrangements that are limited to a one-year term and that do not penalize dealers that subsequently switch suppliers are unlikely to exclude new suppliers from the market. In contrast, an exclusionary effect is more likely where large suppliers' exclusive dealing contracts have very long terms and assess major financial penalties against dealers who change suppliers.

Also relevant is the size of the minimum efficient scale of operations in the supplying or distributing markets as compared with that in the manufacturing market. For example, if the minimum efficient scale of distribution is very large, exclusionary effects are more likely. The Department will take into account the surrounding circumstances of each case in evaluating the duration and restrictiveness of vertical restraint provisions. Depending on the content, particular restrictions may bring about efficiencies in certain market settings but unjustifiably restrain competition in other very different marketplace situations.

4.224   The intent of the parties

On occasion there may be direct evidence of the intent of firms employing restraints, and this may be a good indication of the likely consequences of the practice. For example, if the responsible officials of a firm involved in a vertical restraint adopted it solely to facilitate collusion, that would be a strong indication that suppression of competition is the most likely explanation for the restraint. Evidence indicating an apparent anticompetitive purpose must be evaluated carefully, however, because it may merely be an expression of excessive zeal on the part of low-level employees with little ability to influence corporate decisions or it may simply reflect a purpose to prevail over competitors by lawful means.

4.225 Are restraints used by small firms or new entrants?

If many of the firms employing vertical restraints have small market shares or have entered the market recently (e.g., within the past two years), there is good reason to believe that the restraints in question are not being used for an anticompetitive purpose, unless the restraints were imposed by dominant firms at the adjacent level of distribution. Small firms are unlikely to be using a vertical restraint to exclude larger rivals or to facilitate a collusive scheme. Thus, if small firms use a restraint at their own initiative, the motivation is most likely to be the pursuit of efficiency. If recent entrants employ the restraint, the most likely purpose is to persuade dealers to carry and promote a product—a procompetitive purpose. While a vertical practice may be used for both efficiency and anticompetitive purposes, its voluntary use by new entrants or firms with small market shares makes it more credible that its use by other firms in the market is designed to achieve potential efficiency gains.

4.226 Can the firm or firms engaging in the restraint identify credible procompetitive efficiencies from the practice?

While an inability to demonstrate efficiencies should not be interpreted as proof of an anticompetitive explanation for a restraint (efficiencies may be present but the firms may be unable to demonstrate them), an ability to demonstrate efficiencies that withstand scrutiny indicates that an anticompetitive explanation is less plausible than it would be in the absence of an efficiency justification. For example, an exclusive territorial arrangement justified on the ground that it prevents dealers from free riding is more likely to withstand scrutiny if suppliers can point to promotional activities or other dealer-provided services that are fostered by the existence of exclusive territories.

5. TYING ARRANGEMENTS

5.1 Nature and Effects of Tying

Under a tying arrangement, a seller requires that the buyer of a product[32] purchase a second, distinct product as a condition of purchasing the first. The first product is referred to as the "tying" product and the second product is referred to as the "tied" product.

Tying arrangements often serve procompetitive or competitively neutral purposes. One procompetitive use is to protect the integrity or reputation of a product. Where the manner in which purchasers use a product may affect a manufacturer's reputation and future sales, the manufacturer may ensure that the purchaser maintains desired standards by tying the sale of the product to a maintenance contract or to sales of "approved" parts, and thus reduce the risk of inferior service by distributors.

Another procompetitive use of tying is to redistribute risk. For example, a manufacturer may induce distributors to carry a new product by selling it to them at a low price, while relying on expected sales of some tied item used in conjunction with the new product to generate his profits. The manufacturer, thus, assumes a greater share of the risk that the new product will be rejected by consumers. If the new product proves very popular, the distributors will require many of the related items, and the manufacturer will receive a large reward. If the new product does not succeed, however, the distributors will require very few of the related items and will have to pay very little. This "risk sharing" efficiency may apply to a wide range of licensing, franchising, and similar distributional arrangements that involve tying.

Tying arrangements also have uses that are neither clearly procompetitive nor clearly anticompetitive, such as to achieve

---

32. The term "product" as used in this discussion refers to both goods and services.

price discrimination.[33] Because price discrimination has ambiguous or unpredictable welfare effects (e.g., some consumers may benefit from the practice, while others may be harmed), there is no firm basis for condemning the use of tying to further this goal.

Tying arrangements generally do not have a significant anticompetitive potential. It has been posited that tying arrangements may be used to eliminate independent suppliers of the tied product and thereby exclude rivals who produce the complementary, tying product. The exclusionary effect in such cases flows, however, not from tying but from any exclusive dealing or vertical integration that accompanies the tying. In the absence of exclusive dealing requirements, the supplier of the tying product cannot deprive its rivals' customers of access to other sellers of the tied product. Thus, rival producers of the tying product will be able to compete effectively for customers with the firm employing the tie.

5.2 Judicial Treatment of Tying

The Supreme Court recently held that tying arrangements are illegal per se when (1) the seller has market power in the tying market, (2) the tying and tied products are separate,[34] and (3) there is a substantial adverse effect in the tied product market. *Jefferson Parish Hospital District No. 2 v. Hyde*, 104 S. Ct. 1551 (1984). If the seller does not possess "dominant" market power in the market for the tying product, the tying arrangement will be upheld under the rule of reason, unless it can be proved that the arrangement otherwise unreasonably restrained competition in the market for the tied product.

---

33. For example, where the volume of purchases of a tied good differs according to the intensity of use of the tying product, a tying arrangement may allow heavy users of a product to be charged a higher effective per unit price than infrequent users.

34. The Department does not view tied products as separate unless the "tied" product has a use separate from the "tying" product. Moreover, when the economic advantages of jointly packaging and merchandising two different products are substantial, the products will not be viewed as separate.

5.3 Screen and Competitive Analysis of Tying Arrangements

The Department will employ the following screen in evaluating tying cases:

> The use of tying will not be challenged if the party imposing the tie has a market share of thirty percent or less in the market for the tying product. This presumption can be overcome only by a showing that the tying agreement unreasonably restrained competition in the market for the tied product.

This screen recognizes that where the party imposing a tie has a share of thirty percent or less in the market for the tying product, "dominant"[35] market power does not exist—and the tie is not per se illegal. It recognizes as well that where a tying agreement does not unreasonably or significantly restrain competition in the tied product market, it is legal. In many cases, it may be immediately apparent that a tie has not significantly blunted competition in the tied product market. In such instances, the Department will conclude, without detailed inquiry, that the tie should not be challenged.

If the market share in the tying product market is over 30 percent, the Department will attempt to determine whether the seller has "dominant" market power. Where the seller has dominant power, and the other factors necessary to find a per se violation are present, a tie will be considered per se illegal. In those situations where dominant market power is not present, the Department will apply a rule of reason analysis. Employing this analysis, it will only challenge those ties that unreasonably restrain competition in the tied product market, taking into account the competitive considerations previously described. In short, the mere fact that a seller has more than 30 percent of the

---

35. For purposes of these Guidelines, "dominant" market power refers to a degree of market power in the tying market that approaches monopoly proportions. *See Jefferson Parish Hospital District No. 2 v. Hyde,* 104 S. Ct. 1551, 1559-1561, 1566 (1984).

market for the tying product does not necessarily indicate that the use of tying is anticompetitive.

6. MARKET DEFINITION PRINCIPLES

Using the standards described below, the Department will define the relevant markets at each level of distribution affected by the restraint. These standards are designed to enable the Department to analyze the likely competitive impact of a restraint within economically meaningful markets—i.e., markets in which a firm or firms employing a particular restraint could effectively exercise market power. The group of goods or services (hereinafter "product") and geographic area that comprise a market are referred to respectively as the "product market" and the "geographic market."

6.1 Product Market Definition

Where a vertical restraint involves a single identifiable product or group of products that remain essentially unchanged through the distribution chain, the product market will be the same at each level of distribution. Where, however, a vertical restraint involves an input that is used by the purchaser to manufacture a separate identifiable product for resale or a "tied" or "tying" product, separate product markets will be defined for both levels of distribution.

In defining product markets, the Department will employ the general market definition principles set forth in its Merger Guidelines.[36] At each level of distribution, the Department will begin by considering each, narrowly defined product subject to the restraint under scrutiny. It will then ask what would happen if a hypothetical monopolist of that product imposed a small but significant and nontransitory increase in price. If the price increase would cause so many buyers to shift to other products

---

36. *See* Merger Guidelines § 2.1.

that the price increase would not be profitable for the hypothetical monopolist, the Department will add to the product group the product that is the next best substitute for the product subject to the vertical restraint and ask the same question again. This process will continue until a group of products is identified for which a hypothetical monopolist's price increase would be profitable.

As in the case of analyzing markets for mergers, application of this market definition procedure normally will lead the Department to include more than a single brand of a product in the market. In most cases, there is significant competition among competing brands of a product, and defining a product market to correspond to a single brand of a product would yield unrealistic answers to the Department's economic analysis.

6.2 Geographic Market Definition

Taking into consideration the existence and nature of vertical restraints, the Department also will define the relevant geographic market for each level of the distribution chain. The purpose of geographic market definition is to establish a geographic boundary that roughly separates firms that are important factors in the competitive analysis of a vertical restraint from those that are not.

In defining the geographic market or markets affected by a vertical restraint, the Department will employ the general market definition principles set forth in its Merger Guidelines.[37] At each level of distribution, the Department will begin with the location of each firm employing the restraint under scrutiny and ask what would happen if a hypothetical monopolist of the product subject to the restraint imposed a small but significant and nontransitory price increase at that location. If this action caused so many buyers to shift to products produced in other areas that a hypothetical monopolist producing or selling the relevant product at the firm's location would not find it profit-

---

37. *See* Merger Guidelines § 2.3.

able to impose such an increase in price, the Department will add the location from which production is the next-best substitute for production at the location of the firms subject to restraint and ask the same question again. This process will be repeated until the Department identifies an area in which a hypothetical monopolist could profitably impose a small but significant and nontransitory increase in price.

6.3 Step One v. Step Two

For purposes of the Department's Step One inquiry, it will often be easy quickly to identify in rough terms the relevant geographic and product markets. For example, the product market may be defined as the product or products subject to the restraint and obvious substitutes. The geographic market may often be shaped by existing well-established patterns of distribution channels and territories. Such "quick look" market definition usually will suffice for the Step One inquiry; more refined analysis would defeat the purpose of the "quick look" step.

Step Two, however, sometimes may require a more refined analysis of the relevant market structure and, therefore, a more precise definition of the relevant markets. Therefore, in Step Two, the Department will rely on the market definition approach outlined above, which is essentially the analysis used by the Department in analyzing mergers.

INDEX

A

B

D

Dakin, 67
Data General Corporation, 58–61
Dealer Day in Court Act. *See* Automobile Dealer Franchise Act
Dealers:
    complaints of, 20–21
    selection of, 10–11
    terminations of, 73–87
Department of Justice. *See* Justice Department
Dilution doctrine, 136
Discounters, 11–16, 80
Dual distribution, 32–33, 36

E

Ease of entry, 37–38, 56
Electrical equipment conspiracy, 3, 91
Environmental Protection Agency, 143
Equal Credit Opportunity Act, 157
Exclusive dealerships. *See* Exclusive distributorships
Exclusive dealing, 54–57
Exclusive distributorships, 20, 56–57, 65–67, 76–77

F

Fair Credit Billing Act, 157–58
Fair Credit Reporting Act, 157
Fair Packaging and Labeling Act, 143
Fair Trade Laws, 12
Federal Reserve Board, 156
Federal Trade Commission, 6, 32, 98, 111, 122–28, 131, 143, 155
Federal Trade Commission Act, 6
Financing, 156–58
Food and Drug Administration, 124, 128, 143, 155

L

M

N

O

P

Q

R

U

V

W

Y